John Jacob Ruegg

The Silk Calculator

John Jacob Ruegg

The Silk Calculator

ISBN/EAN: 9783337342586

Printed in Europe, USA, Canada, Australia, Japan

Cover: Foto ©Lupo / pixelio.de

More available books at **www.hansebooks.com**

JACOB WALDER,

188 RIVER STREET.   PATERSON, N. J.

Manufacturer of all kinds of

☀ Reeds, Harnesses, Lingoes, Mails ☀

SHUTTLES AND QUILLS.

· DEALER IN ·

Weavers' Materials in General.

TELEPHONE CALL 30.

WORCESTER, Mass.,

BUILDERS OF

OPEN : SHED : FANCY : LOOMS,

And Every Variety of Weaving Machinery.

We make a Specialty of Looms for

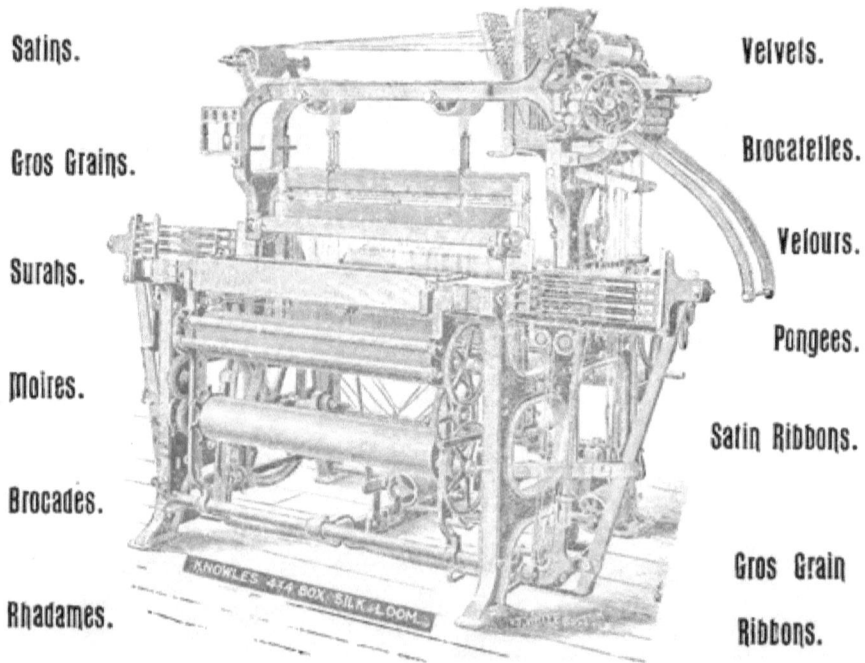

Satins.

Gros Grains.

Surahs.

Moires.

Brocades.

Rhadames.

Velvets.

Brocatelles.

Velours.

Pongees.

Satin Ribbons.

Gros Grain Ribbons.

WE ALSO BUILD

➤ Jaquards, Dobbies, Shedding Engines, Etc. ⬅

SEND FOR CIRCULARS.

Rise-and-Fall 624h.
Rotary Cylinder Jacquard.

Our Rise=and=Fall 624=hook Rotary Cylinder Jacquard

Is at present running in Paterson at 140-picks per minute on broad silks and producing perfect cloth at that speed.

We invite you to inspect this Jacquard at the store of our Paterson Agent, Holden Rigby, Washington and Fair Streets, where we shall be pleased to show you its superior mechanism in actual operation.

Schaum & Uhlinger,
Philadelphia, U. S. A.

calculation there is success.

◁ THE ▷

SILK CALCULATOR

A PRACTICAL MANUAL

FOR

SILK CALCULATIONS

WITH

Yarn Comparative Tables, Weight Tables, Calculations of Silks and Calculation Blanks.

THIRD EDITION

BY

JOHN J. RUEGG,

SUPERINTENDENT FOR GOLDEN ROD SILK COMPANY,

PATERSON, N. J.

PATERSON, N. J.:
CALL PRINTING AND PUBLISHING COMPANY.
1894.

[SECOND EDITION]

PREFACE.

Nothing is more necessary to the Silk Manufacturer than the ability to make up calculations quickly and accurately. To do this, he needs weight tables of warp and filling, out of which he can see at a glance the necessary exact weights.

These tables have been in use by the publisher for a long time and were only reprinted by the special request of some friends in the silk manufacturing trade, who, also would like to use this manual. We know that in general the calculations of silks is very complicated, and that it takes a certain education and experience to calculate without self-delusion, particularly complicated goods. This calculator facilitates our problem considerably by means of the calculation formularies, weight and comparative tables; on the other hand, these tables are of great use to us in the dyeing and warping departments, and will save us much trouble and time in many different ways.

JOHN J. RUEGG.

Paterson, N. J., Dec. 1893.

[THIRD EDITION.]

PREFACE.

The continual demand of this work has shown how practical the "Silk Calculator" in the various manufacturing departments has been found. This third edition has been increased considerably by Comparative Tables, Calculations of Silks in twelve qualities and articles, Yarn Calculations and explanations of decomposition and calculation. The entire work now contains twenty-five tables.

Considering that thick volumes can be written about calculations to explain the thousandfold knowledge gathered by twenty years' experience in decomposition and calculation of plain and very rich fancy goods, this "Silk Calculator" will nevertheless form a good basis to many who intend increasing their knowledge in the silk line, and in many places it is perhaps proper to obtain a more uniform and more rational system of calculation.

THE PUBLISHER.

CONTENTS.

	PAGE.
Explanation of Decomposition and Calculation....	7–17
Yarn Calculations......................	18–21
Calculations of Silks in 12 different articles and qualities........................	23–34
Calculation Blanks...........................	35–110
Warp Weight Table of Raw or Thrown Silk; Length: 100 Yards.................	112–115
Warp Weight Table of Raw or Thrown Silk; Length: 300 Yards.................	116–119
Warp Weight Table of Cotton or Spun Silk Yarns; Length: 100 Yards.................	120–121
Filling Weight Table of Tram; Width: 20 Inches; Length: 100 Yards.................	124–126
Filling Weight Table of Tram; Width: 24 Inches; Length: 100 Yards.................	127–129
Filling Weight Table of Tram; Width: $27\frac{1}{2}$ Inches; Length: 100 Yards.................	130–131
Filling Weight Table of Cotton or Spun Silk Yarns; Width: 24 Inches; Length: 100 Yards;	132
Remarks about Waste........................	133
Comparative Yarn Tables.....................	136–142

THE DECOMPOSITION AND CALCULATION.

THE DECOMPOSITION AND CALCULATION OF SILK IN GENERAL CONSISTS OF TEN PRINCIPAL PARTS.

1. Binders or Armures of the Web.
2. Number of ends per inch, width of cloth and reed.
3. Number of picks per inch.
4. Sizes and weights of the raw materials.
5. Dyeing.
6. Wages in the whole manufacturing process.
7. Harness and eventual designs.
8. Finishing.
9. General Expenses.
10. Selling Expenses.

The manufacture of silk is so very manifold that a large amount of special kind of manufacture can be treated. The object of the Silk Calculator, however, is not to enter upon specialties, but to treat the manufacture of silk in general, and only in as much as it concerns advantageous calculation.

BINDERS OR ARMURES

If we have a sample before us to calculate, we take our familiar counting glass which enlarges the web about 8 times and examine the sample by the ground binders. We see whether the binder is Tabby, Surah or Satin, Armure, combined binders or a Jacquard weave. By means of a needle holder we can specify the exact Armures, for instance, we see in a ¼ inch counting glass on the back of a satin sample, 8 repeats, *i. e.*, 8 thread binders; now we have to decide whether the satin binders are 5, 8, 10 or 12. For this purpose the best would be if we would slowly pull out a thread from the back of the sample and then observe after how many picks it is bound again; if we see that it is again bound after the seventh pick, *i. e.*, 7 floats and 1 binder, it is a satin sample of 8, is the thread only bound after 11 picks it is a satin sample of 12, etc.

In the same manner we analyze Surahs, Twills, Diagonals, Royals, Armures, etc. If we have in a satin sample 8 repeats and the binder is **one of 8**, we have in a quarter of an inch 8x8 = 64 ends or in one inch 4x64 = 256 ends per inch or in 21 inches 21x264 = 5376 ends. All silks weave in or take up more or less, consequently we will have to add 1, 2, or 3 per cent. of the number of ends, so that in above case, the goods are 21 in. wide after weaving. In case goods have special edges we mostly make them as much wider as the number of ends they contain, because in a number of goods, the webs do not weave in more than a quarter of an inch, in some of course ½ inch and more. Special weave and special finish change this rule and in the specification of ends, we have to take into consideration our experience and all circumstances.

After we have the number of ends of the sample in the whole width, we will have to determine the calculation of the reed. If we want to manufacture goods exactly as per sample, we find out the reed best, if we hold the sample and counting glass, in proper manner, up to the broad daylight, and with a little practice, we can see in an instant, that there are always a number of ends together and that between each of these groups of ends there is a very small empty space. In this empty space the dent of the reed has been while weaving. We can then easily determine whether 2, 3, 4, or more ends are together. In a satin of 8 with 256 ends per inch, we can mostly specify 4 ends per dent, what in a reed of 64 dents per inch, is called a "$\frac{4}{4}$".

In certain loose or very rich webs, it is sometimes difficult to see the reed in the weave; an experienced calculator, however, knows his rules and choses his reed mostly around 60 dents per inch and not higher than 80 dents; only in *very few* cases and only for *special* goods he will go as much as 100 dents per inch, the finer the reed, the better the quality of the material and the twist of the silk has to be, and the less picks the goods ought to have.

To determine the number of picks, we again take the counting glass, place it on the back of the sample, very often the best is to put it on the edges and count the picks in a quarter of an inch and in an inch. Is the sample a combined web with different proportions of picks we will have to find out the picks in an inch of each web, so that we can figure it correctly in the calculation of the material.

MATERIALS.

After the calculator has determined warp and filling as far as number of ends and picks are concerned, he has to find out the raw material. He has to determine before anything else, whether there is in a sample Raw or Thrown Silk, Spun, Cotton or Woollen Yarns. Owing to the experience and theory of each educated calculator in regard to material, he can, in an instant determine what it is. To specify them the following rules are worthy of notice:

a) RAW SILK.

This material we know, if we pull out a number of ends out of a sample, by the fineness of the thread, on which we can absolutely find no twist, which therefore by only very little elastic extension opens out into 15, 20 or more fine threads, called cocoon threads. This material we only find in piece-dyed goods and in sizes of 16-18—24-26 deniers. This silk works very advantageous in manufacture.

b) THROWN SILK.

ORGANZINE.

Under Organzine Straffilato we understand a silk twisted together out of two (for special purposes also more) ends in which the single thread receives a turn from right to left of generally 15-16 turns per inch (filato or first twist) the doubled or compound thread a reversed turn from left to right of generally 14-12 turns per inch (torto or second twist). In Organzine Strattorto, or hard twist, the double thread receives 18 turns per inch for filato or first twist and 14 turns per inch for torto or second twist.

Under Organzine moyen appret (medium twist), we understand a silk thread with 12-14 turns per inch for filato or first twist, and 8-10 turns per inch for torto or second twist.

TRAM.

Tram is manufactured by generally doubling two, three, four or more Raw Silk threads to an end and then receiving a slight twist of ordinarily 2 to 3 turns per inch.

RAW OR THROWN SILK

is principally distinguished by its origin (Provenienz) European, Levantine, Asiatic silks with their mostly existing sub-divisions

French, Italian, Spanish, Syrian, Brassia, Nonka, Bengal, China, Canton, Japan and a great number of other gradations according to region and race.

c) SPUN SILK YARN.

This silk is spun out of the cocoon waste, the extreme outer and inner portion of every cocoon being used for spun silk, and cocoons which are in any way soiled or unable to produce a continuous thread. These wastes are called Strozzi.

Of this fine, short material, hundreds of threads, after a preceding special process, according to sizes, are spun together to one.

Spun Silk in the raw is generally yellowish or brownish, silk spun out of China waste is whitish, however; this natural color is imitated in other material by bleaching, which but with a little experience is easily distinguished.

Spun Silk is mostly used in single, for filling for heavy goods, also very often in 2 ply twist as warp, with good quality Spun Silk, brilliant articles can be manufactured.

d) COTTON YARN.

In this material we principally distinguish two kinds. Egyptian and American Cotton.

For cheap articles mostly American in 1 and 2 ply is used, but if we have rich, soft, even and lustrous Dress Silks to manufacture, we exclusively use Egyptian Cotton 1 or 2 ply, for rich Satin Cotton Backs, Bengalines, Serge for linings, etc., this material gives the best result.

SIZES OF RAW OR THROWN SILK.

Sizes of Raw and Thrown Silk we find the surest way in calculating, if we count the cocoon threads, by use of the counting glass. In a raw silk 14-15 deniers we can mostly count 10 to 12 cocoon threads to which we, according to the well known basis, have to add $\frac{1}{4}$ to get the sizes of the deniers. If, for instance, we extract out of a sample 12 ends we establish the sizes as follows:

Organzine, threads   I. II. III. IV. V. VI. VII. VIII. IX. X. XI. XII.
show Cocoon threads 17 18 21 17 23 18 18   19   19 21 17 18.

An average of 18, 7 cocoon threads.
Plus $\frac{1}{4}$ = 6, 3

Total, 25

226 cocoon threads or per 1 Organzine thread 12: 226 Average = 25 deniers or $\frac{25}{18}$ = 1$\frac{1}{2}$ drams organzine.

The second proceeding, which we oftener use in the calculation of sizes, is, that we pull out of a sample to be examined, 24 warp or filling ends and compare these with a seemingly similar, but well known to us, size, in twisted condition and continue the comparison with finer or coarser sizes till we are satisfied with the result, and consequently can calculate, the correct size. The counting of cocoon threads, which takes up so much time, but which is a very good practice, we shall mostly only then make use of, when we have very small samples sent to us to calculate.

The quality of silk in the raw is designated by the color, lustre and hand, also by the cleanliness, evenness, elasticity and strength of the thread. To determine these qualities our eyes and hand, in the first place, serve us, secondly, as mechanical help, the proofs of size, elasticity and strength.

The task of determining the nature of a silk when dyed in a weaved sample, therefore is not so easy, nevertheless we can in case we have good practice at our disposal distinguish High Classical Italian Organzine from other "Provenienzes."

Italian High Classical Organzine we shall mostly use for warps in rich articles, whereas China and Japan Filature Organzine for cheap Tie and Dress Silks and principally for mufflers and handkerchiefs.

For tram in cheap articles nearly exclusively Japan Raw stock is used, as Japan rereels, as well as China and Canton raw stock; the latter is very hairy and in consequence of its unevenness is used for 4, 5 and 6 threads tram of 3 and 4 turns per inch. For very rich or very particular articles Italian Classical raw stock is also often used for 2 thread tram, as we find especially in such a filling evenness, elasticity and cleanliness; we will also very often use best Japan Filatures.

In case we do find in calculating a sample the real nature of a silk, it is not always said that the manufacturer should use the same material. In choosing raw material there is still quite a lot of money thrown away in manufacturing. We see articles manufactured, which give us, with much cheaper raw stock the same goods in quantity, quality and effect, whereas again sometimes pretty nearly the opposite case occurs. If we use cheap material this should not be done at the sacrifice of the production, we run across many articles, in which such material, if treated right in the throwing process, does not display any bad influence at all on the result of the goods. In general we know that nice materials always give better results, but there are in our thousand-fold manufacturing process very many advantageous exceptions, with which we sometimes save very much money.

The material in piece dyed goods we will mostly find for warp as Classical Italian Raw Silk $\frac{20}{22}$, $\frac{24}{26}$, etc., deniers, although Japan Filature best No. 1 is often chosen.

In the material question, no special rules can be made. In choosing same the calculator has to make use of his entire experience, as well as to take into consideration his more or less capable machinery.

In the question about raw material and its sizes, the *real* weight of the raw silk comes into consideration, without giving ourself to any self delusion. We know, that it often happens, that throwsters soak their silk with 5-10 per cent. soap and oil. In case we base our calculation on such silk already soaked by the throwster, the result of the calculation will show no small self delusion, consequently we have to, in a case like this, keep our eye on the kinds of soaked silk, and of course do better if we do the throwing ourselves or have the silk thrown as bright as possible.

DYEING.

According to the appearance of the silk, the calculator has to find out the way of dyeing.

Is warp and filling in colors in a sample very bright and elastical, we suppose it is pure dye, is a filling mat in the color, it is generally weighted $1\frac{1}{4}$ oz.

The rules are, that the blacks for warps are generally weighted $\frac{30}{22}$ oz., i. e. 30 per cent., for special purposes they are also weighted only $\frac{18}{16}$ oz. but also $\frac{24}{26}$ oz., whereas for solid goods, only "pure dye" is used for warp and filling. Colors are generally dyed "pure dye" for warp, for filling often bright $1\frac{1}{4}$ oz., although where it is necessary to give the article a very effective appearance, and it does not depend upon "full hand," pure dye is used. Black bright for filling is generally weighted $\frac{26}{22}$ oz., seldom $\frac{30}{22}$ oz. Souple Colors as well as black, are mostly dyed for Dress Silks, where "full hand" and heavy goods are first condition, colors are mostly weighted $\frac{24}{26}$, $\frac{26}{28}$ oz., at the highest $\frac{30}{22}$ oz. and black mostly $\frac{40}{22}$ oz., i. e. 160 per cent. at the highest $\frac{55}{22}$ oz., i. e. 225 per cent. Souple Silk we know by its mat appearance and very poor elasticity.

It is a well known fact, that for instance, domestic goods are dyed in general much more solid than imported goods. In the weighting of silk, the European dyers accomplish the greatest that can be done and go into extremes to the disadvantage of the solidity of the goods. Considering that the domestic dyer, in comparison to the foreign dyer, has to pay higher wages, the extreme weighting is neither advantageous for the dyer nor for the manufacturer, and consequently the consumer has on domestic goods a perhaps unknown but considerable advantage regarding the solidity of silks.

For dyeing "souple dye," we mostly use best Japan Filature Tram, to obtain a good weight, seldom Italian Tram, nevertheless it happens, but only for special goods. Coarse sizes can also be weighted heavier than fine sizes, for instance, a 2 thread filling can at the most, be weighted $\frac{33}{22}$ oz. in black, whereas 3, 4 and 5 thread 46-50 and 50-55 oz.

WARP AND FILLING WEIGHTS.

When the calculator has fixed the materials and their sizes, he figures their weights for the respective lenghts in warp and filling. In fixing the number of ends we have quoted an example in which our reed is supposed to be $\frac{64}{4}$ in 21 in.; according to this supposition there would be 21x256 = 5356 ends. However, most goods weave in in width according to the weave 2, 3 or 5 per cent., in many articles, we add the number of ends of the edges for weaving in, which can be mostly 120 to 160 double ends = 2x30 to 40 ends for a warp, etc., etc.

Now, if we have in the article in question 5356 ends, in an organzine $\frac{33}{22}$ deniers or $1\frac{1}{2}$ drams Italian Organzine, and the edges eventually of

Classical China Organzine $\frac{17}{19}$ deniers or $2\frac{1}{2}$ drams, it is an easy thing to establish in an instant the weights including waste, by use of the weight tables.

The edges will have to be figured 5 to 10 per cent. longer than the warp according to the quality and kind of web.

The weight tables are for warp 100 and 300 yards long, if we desire to figure the warp eventually 600 yards, for double wide goods 1200 yards, we have to double or quadruple the weights of the 300 yard tables.

The weights of filling can be ascertained just as easily as the weights of warps.

If in a sample the picks per inch are known to us, we multiply the width with the number of picks and length of the warp, and this with the size of the filling, divide by 1000 and 256, the result is lbs.

Example: width, 21 inches
picks per inch, 100
length, 600 yards
filling, $2\frac{1}{2}$ drams

$21 \times 100 = 2100 \times 600 = 1260000 \times 2\frac{1}{2} = 3150000 : 1000 = 3150 : 256 =$ lb lbs. 12 or 1s., $2\frac{30}{100}$. oz. 5.

To this weight of filling, the waste according to the quality, dyeing and nature of the silk will have to be added = 5 to 10 per cent. Then the weaving in, in width and length will have to be taken into consideration. Many articles weave in, 2-3 per cent. in width, and 3-6 per cent. in length, consequently we have to figure as already mentioned, the filling in above example with $21\frac{1}{2}$ inches, and for the length 580 yards at the most, instead of 600 yards for the warp. Mostly, however, we figure on the weaving in equalizing itself in width and length; this is not correct under certain circumstances, however, practice mostly chooses the favorable side if it comes to trifles.

WAGES.

The American silk industry, in consequence of high wages and large competition with all European places like Switzerland, Italy, Spain, France, Germany, Austria, England and also Japan, is forced to prepare itself with the utmost energy for the most imaginable and most advantageous manufacture; no stone is left unturned to render the greatest ability in every manufacturing department; the American manufacturer continually improves his machinery, no trouble and money is saved in this direction. The better the machinery in a mill the more it can produce in better and cheaper articles.

Nowhere it pays less than here to carry a large variety of articles and always to change, as it is done in European places. Here a manufacturer sticks to his staple articles as long as he can and the principle of quantity is made best of in the highest degree. Anybody who tries to swim against the stream can not possibly be successful.

Now, if we want to figure on the cheapest possible wages we have to in the first place consider the most important factor, raw material. If we keep material, that works without any trouble during the manufacturing process, we are sure of a good result in our calculation. If we do not strictly carry out the principle of raw material, we are mostly deceived in some point in the calculation and the goods rather come higher than cheaper, the general expenses are rather unfavorable than favorable, the delivery time is rather later than earlier and workman, manufacturer and sellers are rather dissatisfied than satisfied.

THROWING.

Nowhere the advantage of good material shows itself as well as in this division of manufacture; we can run all machines with the highest speed and it pays to have in a very short while the best machinery. European throwsters are not little surprised, when they see the high speed American throwing machines, and when they see that our spinners run-

For first twist 9,000 revolutions.

For second twist 7,500 revolutions.

Of course there are exaggerations in this direction, by some machines being forced to 14,000 revolutions. Everything, also in good material has its boundary and just for the reason, in this case, to get a more even twist which is impossible and in every case disadvantageous if carried out to an extreme. If we desire to have our throwing machines run to an advantage, we generally only throw in few sizes and avoid altogether, fine silk as raw silk $\frac{9}{16}$ $\frac{10}{12}$, a great many manufacturers have their Organzine thrown $\frac{13}{14}$ and $\frac{13}{15}$ deniers and Tram $\frac{13}{15}$ and $\frac{14}{15}$ deniers.

SOFT SILK WINDING.

For this work, we can render in this department with the latest winding frames in comparison to the former system a large advantage in capacity. We know, that European winding frames are equipped with three spindles, one behind the other and that all silk is wound from the skein on the first spindle and bobbin, then from the second spindle and bobbin to the third spindle and bobbin. This running over is done to give the silk thread an even extension and to obtain good bobbins for the warpers. This work is not done by the American manufacturer in the same manner, and very seldom, and out of the simple reason, because this expensive work taking up so much time is less necessary on account of the use of strong extra classical material. If we think this rewinding or running over, necessary, we do not have this work done on winding frames by good paid winders, but on special draw sides and use cheap labor

If we have a particularly exact article or a lot spoiled in dying or a bad winding lot we have the silk wound twice.

The most capable winding frame, in regard to quantity and space, for good material is the well known Double Deck Winding Frame, which is in our calculation undoubtedly 15-20 per cent. in our favor.

Quill winding is mostly done for pure dye colors, light weighted and Cotton Spun Silk Fillings, etc., on "English Quillers," whereas heavy weighted fillings in black or colors, can only be quilled advantageously on "French Quillers."

WARPING.

The warping process has a very great significance and so we can say well considered, warped well, is half woven. The principle, of course, is shown in many different ways and that is why we have for warping so many different systems.

The most rational, best and at the same time cheapest system is the Horizontal Warping Mill, but everybody has his own opinion about this, therefore we see in many factories only horizontal warpers, in others only the well known Swiss warping mills and in many factories both are used according to the quality of the goods.

Undoubtedly the horizontal warping mills are the most advantageous in regard to capacity as they can furnish in the same space of time 2 to 3 times as many warps as possibly can be made on a Swiss mill, therefore the making of such a warp is much cheaper.

For certain articles the horizontal warps are picked as good as possible in beaming and to avoid the well known trouble of the "section marks" the warp is again run back over the mill and again beamed.

This warping system, however, is not the most advantageous, it is and can be correct for some articles, for the bulk, however, this system furnishes uncontrollable warp and not absolutely the best warp for the weavers and all articles.

The most rational warping system in regard to quantity and quality and cheapness is the following :

The warps on horizontal mills are made with a creel of 400 to 500 bobbins about 600, 700 or 800 yards long, beamed at once without being picked and then put on a power warp picking frame. In these very long stretched frames another cross besides the one already existing is made, the whole warp put through a reed, carefully picked, event. Soft and split ends, etc., removed and in 2 days with good material a 600 yard warp is improved in such a way as no warping mill can do, which is a great advantage for the quality of the goods and the weaving wages.

In the well known Swiss warping system there is slowness and incompleteness, or only with first-class and experienced hands the warps are more or less perfect, but still very expensive.

If we know how to introduce the most rational warping system in its greatest perfectness, we save thousands of dollars not only direct, but also indirect by cheap weaving wages and besides this we also have the absolute advantage of much more perfect goods and capacity. Horizontal warping mills have a reel of 8, 10 or 12 yards circumference and the warping is mostly done by men, but can also without hesitation be accomplished by girls and women.

In certain manufacturing towns, part of this warping system has already been introduced, but warps were only picked with an ordinary cross and on hand frames, which system was slow, imperfect and expensive. Only in the perfect system there is quickness, cheapness and superiority and the most imaginable favorable calculation.

WEAVING.

Warped well is half woven in regard to quality, quantity and wages. To this factor, we still need, to obtain the most favorable wages, high speed looms.

If we have good power, excellent looms, good Jacquard machines, best material, a favorable calculation is most certain, if all this is missing, more or less, our calculation is certainly a self delusion and an unsuccessful work from A to Z.

Our looms are mostly made 7 to 6 feet long or in many places even only 5 feet long; the length of the loom has of course great influence on the elasticity of the silk, that is the reason why looms can be seen 8½ to 9 feet long in Europe in the manufacture of fine silk. If we set much value upon space we put a loom every 6, or at the most 7 feet, for Jacquard work, however, with such short looms it is frequently overlooked to choose the most rational Jacquard machine.

For short looms undoubtedly the most rational Jacquard machine, which allows the least shed for Yarn dyed warps is the "Rotary Rise and Fall Jacquard" Machine. This Jacquard saves money in regard to the use of the harnesses, quality of silk and can be run very easily 124-128 picks per minute.

For high speed Jacquard work, piece dyed goods, we frequently use a double lift, double cylinder Jacquard machine, which will give very good satisfaction for the calculation of mufflers and handkerchiefs, etc.

These Jacquards run first rate up to 160 picks per minute, in general a rapidity of 140 picks per minute is already quite excellent and excels all other systems in capacity. For certain articles:

The ordinary single lift Jacquard Rotary Cylinder
" " double " " "

is used, and same can work excellently up to 110 and 120 picks per minute according to article and silk. All these splendid machines make our calculation much cheaper; good long warps, high speed looms and Jacquards give us in weaving at least an advantage of 25 to 30 per cent. in calculating.

PICKING.

Picking we call the next following work after weaving. Every piece is put on a picking frame, all weaving imperfections removed as good as possible, cleaned from loose ends, etc., and eventually rubbed.

40 to 50 inch goods are mostly picked on power picking frames, while narrow goods are picked on hand frames; experience teaches us, however, that the power picking frames render us undoubtedly an advantage of 30 per cent. in wages.

FINISHING.

The more perfect the finish the better the appearance of the goods, therefore we cannot speak about any saving in this division. Many goods must be singed, rubbed, finished and refinished, if we try to save and omit either one of these treatments, this omission would only be made at the sacrifice of the quality of the goods, and consequently at the sacrifice of the price.

The more perfect finish the goods have, the more salable we make them and we cannot be attentive and strict enough in this direction.

HARNESSES.

The calculation of the harness and reed is done in different ways, one manufacturer figures the harness for 1, 2 or 3 warps and therefore figures the respective amount. This calculation of course depends greatly on the resp. article, loom, loom-fixing and event. Jacquard; if we have excellent looms, and "head motions," or dobbies, we can weave in a shaft harness 6 to 10 warps 600 yards each, if we have cheap looms it can happen according to the articles that the harness has to be replaced after 1,500 to 2,000 yards. Jacquard Harnesses are very expensive, with good machines we ought to run them with the heaviest articles, if they are built rational, 2,000 yards, in light articles, treated well, we ought to be able to extend the capacity in staple articles from 5,000 to 6,000 yards.

In staple goods Harnesses are used for 6-10 warps till they are worn out, and consequently at least $\frac{1}{6}$ of the Harness and Reed expense will have to be figured in the calculation. French Harnesses of 8,000 mails each, passing or entering and reeding cost about $15.00; if we divide this amount on 6 warps the Harness expenses for a calculation would only amount to $2.50. A Jacquard Harness of 8000 mails or lingoes costs complete about $72.00. If we figure $\frac{1}{6}$ of this amount for such warp of about 600 yards the harness and reed expenses for a calculation would be $12.00.

Novelty Harnesses in plain and Jacquard we must, of course, figure on short time and mostly take the full cost in the calculation.

DESIGNING.

Pattern expenses, we distribute in calculating mostly on the respective order, if there are 600 yards ordered of a pattern, we distribute this expense on the number of yards, are only 100 yards ordered we have to figure the same way, which in this case of course, makes the article considerably more expensive. There is also much saving in advantageous drawing and according to a certain drawing proceeding, in patterns, 50 per cent. can be saved in many cases. In a large amount of patterns much money and time can be saved as no ground binders, are they, Tabby Satins or Armures, have to be drawn in case the card cutter knows his business and is instructed in such considerable saving.

In correct rational drawing, the calculation of a design is often 30 to 50 per cent. cheaper.

GENERAL EXPENSES.

This division comprises the following expenses:
1. Annual interest and repairs on mills or rents.
2. Power.
3. Machinery repairs.
4. " fixing.
5. " and factory cleaning.
6. Salaries of bookkeepers and foremen.
7. Stationary expenses.
8. Amortization of machinery, fixtures, furniture, etc.
9. Interest of active capital.

10. Taxes and insurances.
11. Freight Expenses.
12. Management.

If we figure with other calculators simply to experiment, we can frequently see, that the general expenses are fixed in many different ways. Many are under the impression, that they can work with their buildings and machines for decenniums and therefore only take a very small amount as amortization, many again make a mistake in figuring the expenses for loom fixing, interest, taxes, freight, etc.

The correct specification must contain every expense as above mentioned, then the annual net sales must be ascertained and according to this statement the general expenses have to be figured.

A great many manufacturers figure according to their experience and articles 15 per cent. for general expenses.

If a manufacturer produces among others, very advantageous articles, he will, as such articles bring large quantities sometimes go lower than 10 per cent. for general expenses, or if he manufactures less favorable articles slow and awkward to manufacture he will have to go as high as 15 to 20 per cent. for general expenses.

The specification of annual expenses and production and their respective percentages shall only serve the calculator as basis and according to quantity and quality the calculators must either lower or raise his percentage. In many mills we see comparatively very high general expenses, if we look for the reason, we see above all old cheap machinery, which need comparatively many hands, we see inferior raw materials in the manufacturing process, imperfect power, find insufficient capital, which prevent rational improvements in this manner and in consequence thereof inferior capacity; the general expenses are large and the production small so that the calculation can rise higher than to 15 per cent.

But if we put our entire energy on rational management and capacity and figure in every calculation a regular percentage for General Expenses our result can only be favorable and if in full running order we ought to in this account make savings compared to the estimates.

SELLING EXPENSES.

To figure the sale price of an article, the calculator has to figure the selling expenses. These consist of discounts, which the customer demands, salaries of salesmen, as well as interest of capital invested, advertisements, rents, traveling expenses, and insurances, etc., etc., or of commission, which has to be paid to the commission house.

In the entire manufacturing process, we can, by rational machines and management, reduce the cost price considerably; if, however, we want to enjoy the fruits of this improved capability, our goods must be sold by energetic, industrious and earnest salesmen. Both parties must work hand in hand. Wise, rational, cheap and good manufacture, wise, rational, quick sale, and this calculation, with all these best factors combined, must lead every mill to sure success.

YARN CALCULATIONS.

CLASSIFICATIONS OF YARNS USED IN THE MANUFACTURE OF SILKS.

The sizes of yarns are based in the different raw materials upon the number of yards per lb. The number of yards changes according to the respective material, the higher the figure of the number the finer the yarn, except in Raw Silk, where it is just the opposite.

SILK YARNS.

a) SPUN SILK.

Spun Silk Yarns have 840 yards per hank, and are arranged according to the number of hanks per lb. (avoirdupois). Therefore, if 30 hanks, or 30x840 yards = 25200 yards are necessary to make one lb., we say that the yarn is No. 30. If 60 hanks, or 60x840 or 50400 yards are necessary to balance one lb., this thread is a 60 yarn. Spun Silks for filling are mostly used 1 ply, for warps only 2 ply, and for No. $1\frac{20}{2}$, for instance, 2 threads No. 200 are twisted together. No. $1\frac{20}{2}$ has 84000 yards in 1 lb., or 5250 yards in one oz. = 16 drams. Spun Silk or Chappe in French sizes has a standard of 100,000 meters = 1 kilo. A French spun silk yarn No. $1\frac{20}{1}$ has 120,000 meters to the kilo; a yarn No. $2\frac{20}{2}$ ply has 100,000 yards to the kilo.

b) RAW SILK.

The standard basis for raw or thrown silk, is the dram per 1000 yards and in this way, that if a hank or 1000 yards would weigh 1 dram, such a silk is called a 1 dram silk. For Organzine 20000 yard skeins are generally made. If for instance, such a skein weighs 35 drams, such an Organzine would be called a $1\frac{3}{4}$ dram silk. Coarse numbers, for instance Trams, are frequently made in 10000 yards skeins, if such a skein would weigh 3 ounces and 2 drams = 50 drams, such silk would be called a 5 dram silk. The size of raw or thrown silk is always understood in its raw condition including Gum, for instance, the silk loses in boiling off or dyeing, according to its nature from 20 to 30 per cent. China Silks lose most, then Italian, and Japan the least.

In the Italian scale, the fineness of the silk is specified by the "titre." This is designated by the number of deniers a hank of a certain length weighs. Of the different systems the most used, and in cases of dispute the most reliable, is the titolo legale italiano.

A skein of silk of 400 meters long, wound in 400 turns on a swift of $112\frac{1}{2}$ centimeters in circumference, and weighed with a unit of five centigramm (called denier) forms the basis of the titolo legale.

By the following reductions we obtain the result according to the old systems:

100 deniers titolo legale = 103.70 old Milan deniers
"   "   "   "   = 99.117 " Turin   "
"   "   "   "   = 99.583 " Lyons   "

The international titre accepted by the International Congresses in Vienna, Brussels and Turin, and lawfully acknowledged by Germany, is based upon a hank of silk of 500 meters long, reeled in 400 turns of 125 centimeters and weighed with a denier of 5 centigramm. The old Milan deniers have as standard a hank of 476 metres (400 turns at 119 centimetres). Such a denier is = 0,511 grams, and is still sized up to date in many conditioning works, principally in the London conditioning works.

COTTON YARN.

Cotton yarns have same as spun silk as standard per hank 840 yards per lb.

If therefore 60 hanks or 60x840 yards = 50,400 yards are necessary to make 1 lb., we call such a size a No. 60, if only 20 hanks of 840 yards or 20x840 = 16800 yards are necessary, we have a No. 20.

The classification of cotton yarns in 2 ply varies in comparison to those of Spun Silk. In Spun Silk 2 threads of 100 are twisted together for $\frac{50}{2}$ ply, for *Cotton Yarn* 2 threads No. 50 are twisted together for $\frac{50}{2}$ ply.

In No. 40 Cotton Yarn single we have 33,600 yards per lb., whereas in $\frac{40}{2}$ we only have half the length = 16800 yards. No. 100 single has 84,000 yards per lb., in double = $\frac{100}{2}$ only 42000 yards.

FIGURING OF WEIGHTS.

To find the weight in ounces of a known number of yards in a known size the following rules are worthy of notice:

Multiply a given number of yards with 16 and divide the result with the number of yards of the known necessary No. to balance 1 lb.

Example: What is the weight of 21000 yards of $\frac{50}{2}$ Cotton Yarn?
21000x16 = 336000; 1 lb. No. 50 = 42,000, 336000 : 42000 = 8.

Result: 21000 yards of No. 50 weigh 8 oz.

Example: What is the weight of 21000 yards of $\frac{50}{2}$ Cotton Yarn?
21000x16 = 336000; 1 lb. No. $\frac{50}{2}$ = 21000, 336000 : 21000 = 16.

Result: 21000 yards of No. $\frac{50}{2}$ weigh 16 oz.

Following is another rule:

Divide the given number of yards by the number of yards of the known necessary size to 1 oz. (that is per lb., 16).

Example: What is the weight of 21000 yards of No. $\frac{50}{1}$ Cotton Yarn?
42000 : 16 = 2625 yards. No. $\frac{50}{1}$ ply = 1 oz.
21000 : 2625 = 8.

Result: 21000 yards No. $\frac{50}{1}$ weigh 8 oz.

Example: What is the weight of 420000 yards of No. $\frac{100}{2}$ Cotton Yarn?
84000 : 16 = 5250 yards. No. $\frac{100}{2}$ = 1 oz.
420000 : 5250 = 80.

Result: 420000 yards of No. $\frac{100}{2}$ weigh 80 oz. or 5 lbs.

Another rule to find the weight in lbs. of Cotton Yarn of a given number of yards of a known size is:

Divide the given yards by the number of yards of a known size necessary for 1 lb.

Example: What is the weight of 2,520,000 yards of No. $\frac{30}{1}$ Cotton Yarn?
No. $\frac{30}{1}$ = 25200 yards per 1 lb.
2,520,000 : 25200 = 100.

Result: 2,520,000 yards of No. $\frac{30}{1}$ weigh 100 lbs.

Example: What is the weight of 2,520,000 yards of No. $\frac{30}{2}$ Cotton Yarn?
No. $\frac{30}{2}$ = 12600 yards per 1 lb.
2,520,000 : 12600 = 200.

Result: 2520000 yards of No. $\frac{30}{2}$ weigh 200 lbs.

NOTE.—Twisted Yarns can consist of 2, 3 or more, single threads. The more twist and the coarser the yarn the more shrinkage will occur, by one thread being twisted around the other in throwing. If we have, for instance, for fancy yarns a yarn No. 200 twisted together with a No. 10 we obtain a loss, that is a shorter amount of yards than if we twist 2 threads No. 200 together or we have in this case in this fine yarn in proportion more shrinkage than in the coarse yarn. Exact rules for shrinkage in 2 and 3 ply yarn cannot be fixed in so simple a manner as they vary greatly and such a table would require an indefinite number of rules according to sizes, quality of raw materials, tensions, and turns of twist per inch; such rules would therefore be of little use to the manufacturer and in this case we mostly take our experience into consideration.

WOOLLEN YARNS.

a) "RUN" SYSTEM.

Woollen yarns are classified by "runs", which have as standard 1600 yards. This basis is generally known in this way, (except in a few mills in Philadelphia.)

1 "run" yarn of 1600 yards is 1 lb., 5 "run" yarns of 8000 yards 1 lb., 10 "run" yarns = 16000 yards are 1 lb., etc.

In the "run" system, not only same as in Cotton or Spun Silk, whole numbers are counted, but also $\frac{1}{2}$, $\frac{1}{4}$ and even $\frac{1}{8}$, that is:

200 yards = $\frac{1}{8}$ run.
400 yards = $\frac{1}{4}$ " etc., etc.

FIGURING OF A GIVEN NUMBER OF YARDS IN WOOLLEN YARN OF A KNOWN SIZE IN THE "RUN" SYSTEM.

The basis of the "run" facilitates the calculation of Woollen Yarns considerably, as the standard numbers are equivalent with 100 times the number of ounces a lb. contains, so that by multiplying the size of the yarn in "run" counts with 100, and dividing the product into the number of given yards, the result is equivalent to the weight to be found.

Example: What is the weight of 10800 yards of 6 "run" yarn?
6 x 100 = 600.   10800 : 600 = 18.

Result: 10800 yards 6 "run" yarn weigh 18 oz.

Example: What is the weight of 45000 yards in 15 "run" woollen yarn?
45000 : 1500 = 30.

Result: 45000 yards of 15 "run" yarn weigh 30 oz.

b) "CUT" SYSTEM.

In woollen yarns there is another division called the "cut" system.

The basis is 300 yards, that is 300 yards equal 1 lb., or 1 "cut" yarn: 3000 yards = 10 cut yarns, 30000 yards = 100 cut yarns.

The rule, to find the weight in ounces is similar to that of Cotton yarn.

Multiply the given yards by 16, divide the result by the original quantity of yards for the given size of cotton yarn, which contains 1 lb.

Example: What is the weight of 21000 yards of 70 "cut" woolen yarn?
        21000x16 = 336000.
        1 lb. of 70 cut = 21000 yards
        336000 : 21000 = 16.

Result: 21000 yards of 70 cut woollen yarn weighs 16 oz.

2 ply Woollen Yarns are frequently manufactured and they contain half the number of yards as the respective sizes in single ply.

Therefore, a 2 ply 40 "run" woollen yarn is equal to a single 20 "run", each yarn contains 32000 yards or a lb.

A double twist 15 "run" woollen yarn is equal to a $7\frac{1}{2}$ "run" single, and both contain 12000 yards per lb.

WORSTED YARNS.

The standard of worsted yarns is 560 yards to the hank. The number of hanks to balance one pound is the number or count of the yarn. If 80 hanks of 560 yards weigh 1 lb, such a yarn is called a No. 80. If 60 hanks are required to balance one pound, it is known as a No. 60 worsted.

Worsted yarn is used very often in 2 ply. In such a case, only one-half the number of yards is needed to balance the pound of 2-ply yarn. No. $\frac{80}{2}$ requires 28000 yards per lb. and No. 100 2-ply also requires 28,000 yards per pound.

No. $\frac{70}{2}$ worsted has 39200 yards per pound and corresponds to single No. 35.

Rules for finding weights of worsted yarns in ounces.

Example in single yarn: What is the weight of 25200 yards of No. 80 ?
        25200x16 = 403200. One pound of No. 80 = 44800 yards, e. i.
        403,200 : 44800 = 9.

Result: 25200 yards of No. 80 weigh 9 ozs.

Example in 2-ply yarn : What is the weight of 25200 yards of No. $\frac{80}{2}$?
        25200x16 = 403200. One pound of $\frac{80}{2}$ = 22400 yards. Hence
        403200 : 22400 = 18 oz.

Result: 25200 yards of No. $\frac{80}{2}$ weigh 18 ozs.

Example for 3-ply yarn. What is the weight of 25200 yards in No. $\frac{80}{3}$ worsted ?
        25200x16 = 403200. One pound of $\frac{80}{3}$ = $14933\frac{1}{3}$ yards, thus
        403200 : $14933\frac{1}{3}$ = 27.

Result: 25200 yards of No. $\frac{80}{3}$ weigh 27 ozs., or 1 lb. 11 oz.

Rule for finding weights of worsted yarns in pounds.

Example in single yarn : What is the weight of 2520000 yards of No. 80 ?
        One pound of $\frac{80}{1}$ = 44800 yards. Thus, 2520000 : 44800 = $56\frac{1}{4}$.

Result: 2520000 yards of No. $\frac{80}{1}$ = $56\frac{1}{4}$ pounds.

Example in 2-ply yarn. What is the weight of 2520000 yards of No. $\frac{80}{2}$?
        One pound of $\frac{80}{2}$ = 22400 yards. Hence, 2520000 : 22400 = $112\frac{1}{2}$.

Result: 2520000 yards $\frac{80}{2}$ worsted weigh $112\frac{1}{2}$ pounds.

Calculation of TAFFETAS GLACE.

Warp 600 Yards. Cloth 570 Yds. Reed $\frac{40}{0}$. Picks 80. Width 20 In.

	LBS.	OZ.	AT	$	C.
4300 Ends, 1½ dram.					
Organzine, Ital. Extra	18	4	5 00	91	25
Tram, Japan Extra, $\frac{13}{2}$ 3 th.					
2 Filling–5 drams	20		4 20	82	
Dyeing, pure dye	38	4	30	11	49
Winding dyed weight	31		12	3	72
Doubling	16		5	0	80
Quilling	16		12	1	92
Warping, 4500 unpicked			70	3	15
Beaming and Picking				3	15
Twisting				1	15
Weaving 570 Yds.			7	39	90
Picking 570 Yds.			1¼	7	12
Finishing 570 Yds.			1½	8	55
Harness and Reed 6 shafts	½			2	
Designing, Etc.					
General Expenses, 12 %				29	91
570 Yds. cost $				286	11

1 Yard costs net - - - - $	50	
Discount, Com. and Interest, 15 %	9	
85 per 100	59	
Addition 5 %, 95 per 100	3	
Sale Price, per yard - -	62	

Calculation of SURAH FIGURED. Changeable.

Warp 600 Yds. Cloth 570 Yds. Reed ⁹⁰⁄. Picks 84. Width 20 In.

	LBS.	OZ.	AT	$	C.
2460 Double Ends, 1½ dram					
Organzine, Jap. Extra	21	4	60	96	60
Tram, Jap. No. 1, 4¼ dram	18	4	10	73	80
Dyeing, pure dye	39		30	11	70
Winding, dyed weight	32	12	12	3	84
Quilling	18	12	12	2	16
Warping, 4820 ends un-picked			70	3	44
Beaming and Picking				3	44
Twisting				1	25
Weaving 570 yards			10	57	
Picking 570 yards			1	5	70
Finishing 570 yards			1½	8	55
Harness and Reed for Jacquard		½		6	
Designing, Etc., 300 cards			4	12	
General Expenses 15 %				41	80
570 Yards costs $				327	28
1 Yard costs net				57	
Discount, Com. and Interest, 15 %, 85 per 100				10	
				67	
Addition, 5 %, 95 per 100				4	
Sale Price per yard $				71	

Calculation of DUCHESSE BLACK.

Warp 400 Yds. Cloth 380 Yds. Reed $\frac{5}{4}$. Picks 92. Width, 24 In.

	LBS.	OZ.	AT	$	C.
10000 Ends 25 den. or 1½ drm					
Organzine Ital. Extra	25	5		125	
Tram Jap. Extra $\frac{18}{8}$ 3 thr'ds					
2 Filling–5¼ drams	20	4	20	84	
Dyeing Org. $\frac{20}{22}$ oz.	25		90	22	50
Dyeing, Tram Souple 32 oz.	20	1	20	24	
Winding Black Org.	32		12	3	84
Winding Black Souple	40		8	3	20
Quilling and Doubling	40			5	20
Warping, 10,300 ends un-picked			50	5	15
Beaming and Picking				5	15
Twisting				2	60
Weaving, 380 yards			16	60	80
Picking, 380 yards			1½	5	70
Finishing 380 yards			2	7	60
Harness and Reed, 8 Shafts		½		3	20
Designing, etc.					
General expenses, 12 %				42	93
380 Yds. cost $				400	87
1 Yard costs net				1	05
Discount, Com, and Interest 15 %. 85 per 100					18
				1	23
Additions 5 %					7
Sale Price, per yard			$	1	30

Calculation of RHADAME'S Colors.

Warp 600 Yds. Cloth 580 Yds. Reed $\frac{60}{4}$. Picks 92. Width 22 In.

	LBS.	OZ.	AT	$	C.
8500 Ends $\frac{26}{30}$ den. or $1\frac{2}{7}$ dru					
Organzine Ital. Extra	36	5		180	
Tram Jap. Extra, $\frac{14}{15}$, 3 threads					
2 Filling—$5\frac{1}{4}$ drams	24	4	20	100	80
Dyeing Org. pure dye.	36		30	10	80
Tram Souple $\frac{20}{22}$ oz.	24		50	12	
Winding	66		12	7	92
Doubling	30		6	1	80
Quilling	30		12	3	60
Warping 8,500 Ends			70	5	95
Beaming and Picking				5	95
Twisting				4	12
Weaving 580 yards			16	92	80
Picking 580 yards			$1\frac{1}{2}$	8	70
Finishing 580 yards			2	11	60
Harness and Reed 12 Shafts	$\frac{1}{4}$			3	
Designing, Etc.					
General Expenses 12 %				53	88
580 Yds. cost $				502	92
1 Yard costs net			86		
Discount, Com. and Interest, 15 %, 85 per 100			16		
		1	02		
Addition 5 %, 95 per 100			6		
Sale Price per yard $		1	08		

Calculation of SATIN MERVEILLEUX, Piece Dyed.

Warp 600 Yds. Cloth 582 Yds. Reed $\frac{40}{36}$. Picks 84. Width 21 In.

	LBS.	OZ.	AT	$	C.
7600 Ends					
Raw Silk Ital. Extra $\frac{5|4}{|6}$	27	8	3 80	104	50
Spun Silk No. $\frac{50}{1}$ or $9\frac{1}{2}$ drams, on cops	45	12	2 50	114	38
Dyeing, in the piece					
Sky Blue 582 yards			4	23	28
Winding	27	8	10	2	75
Quilling					
Warping 7600 ends picked			80	6	08
Beaming					
Twisting 7600 ends				1	90
Weaving 582 yards			8	46	56
Picking				5	82
Finishing 582 yards			2	11	64
Harness and Reed $\frac{1}{6}$				2	50
Designing, Etc.					
General Expenses 12 %				38	09
582 Yards cost $				358	40
1 Yard costs net - - -			62		
Discount, Com. and Interest, 15 %, 85 per 100			11		
			73		
Addition 5 %, 95 per 100			4		
Sale Price per yard - - - $			77		

Calculation of ARMURE BLACK.

Warp 600 Yds. Cloth 580 Yds. Reed 1/0. Picks 88. Width, 20 In.

	LBS.	OZ.	AT		$	c.
6090 Ends, 3⅜ deniers or 1½ d.						
Organzine Ital. Extra	26		5	00	130	00
Tram Jap. best No. 1 3½ dram	15	8	4	10	63	55
Dyeing, Org. ⅔ oz.	26			90	23	40
Dyeing Souple 1⁰⁄₄ oz.	15	8	1	65	25	57
Winding of Org.	33			12	3	96
Winding of Souple	39			8	3	12
Quilling					2	40
Warping, unpicked 6090 ends				70	4	26
Beaming and Picking					4	26
Twisting					1	55
Weaving 580 Yards				10	58	
Picking 580 Yards				1½	8	70
Finishing 580 Yards				2	11	60
Harness and Reed, ⅛					2	30
Designing, Etc.						50
General Expenses, 12 ⁰⁄₀					40	44
580 Yds. cost $					383	11
1 Yard costs net - - - -				66		
Discount, Com. and Interest, 15 % 85 per 100				11		
				77		
Addition 5 %, 95 per 100				4		
Sale Price, per yard - - - $				81		

Calculation of PONGEE FIGURED. Piece Dyed.

Warp 1000 Yds. Cloth 940 Yds. Reed $\frac{55}{1}$. Picks 84. Width 22 In.

	LBS.	OZ.	AT	$	C.
2750 Double Ends, $\frac{24}{26}$ den. or $1\frac{1}{2}$ dram					
Raw Silk, Ital. Classical	30	3	75	112	50
Tram, $\frac{18}{12}$, 3 threads					
Japan No. 1, $2\frac{3}{8}$ drams	20	4	10	82	
Dyeing, in the piece					
940 yards		4		37	40
Winding	50		10	5	
Quilling	20		10	2	
Warping 4900 ends un-picked				4	90
Beaming and Picking				4	90
Twisting				1	24
Weaving 940 Yds.		8		75	20
Picking 940 Yds.		1		9	40
Finishing 940 Yds.		$1\frac{1}{2}$		14	10
Harness and Reed for Jacquard	$\frac{1}{4}$			9	
Designing, Etc., 300 Cards		4		12	
General Expenses, 12 %				44	10
940 Yds. cost $				413	74
1 Yard costs net				44	
Discount, Com. and Interest, 15 %. 85 per 100				7	
				51	
Addition 5 %, 95 per 100				3	
Sale Price, per yard $				54	

Calculation of GLORIA. Silk Mixed Wool.

Warp 1000 Yds. Cloth 950 Yds. Reed ⁵⁰⁄₁₀. Picks 140. Width 42 In.

	LBS.	OZ.	AT	$	c.
8000 Ends ⅔¼ deniers or 1½ drams					
Raw Silk class. Italian	48	3	80	182	40
Filling Worsted, No. 76 single, best quality	150	1	30	195	
Dyeing in the piece 950 yards			7	66	50
Winding	48	10		4	80
Quilling.					
Warping 8000 ends unpicked				8	
Beaming and Picking				6	
Twisting				2	
Weaving 950 yards.			12	114	
Picking 950 yards.			1	9	50
Finishing 950 yards.			3	28	50
Harness and Reed ¼				5	
Designing, Etc.					
General Expenses 12 %				74	60
950 Yards costs $				696	30
1 Yard costs net,			$	73	
Discount, Com. and Interest 15 %				13	
85 per 100				86	
Addition 10 % 90, per 100				9	
Sale price, per yard			$	95	

Calculation of ARMURE Dress Silk.

Warp 600 Yds. Cloth 570 Yds. Reed ⁵⁵/₅. Picks 100. Width 21 In.

	LBS.	OZ.	AT	$	C.
2900 Ends, 3 drams					
Spun Silk No. 1⁰⁰/₂	22	3	20	70	40
Raw Silk Canton Filature					
⁴⁰/₄₇ deniers or 3¼ drams	19	3		57	
Dyeing, in the piece 570 yards			4	22	80
Winding	41	10		4	16
Quilling	19	10		1	90
Warping 2900 Ends			70	2	03
Beaming and Picking				2	03
Twisting					75
Weaving 570 yards			9	51	30
Picking 570 yards			1	5	70
Finishing 570 yards			2	11	40
Harness and Reed for Jacquard		½		6	
Designing, Etc., 200 Cards			4	08	
General Expenses, 12 %				30	68
570 Yds. cost $				274	09
1 Yard costs net			48		
Discount, Com. and Interest 15 %, 85 per 100			9		
			57		
Addition 5 %, 95 per 100			3		
Sale Price per yard . . . $			60		

Calculation of BROCADES. Three Colors.

Warp 300 Yds. Cloth 280 Yds. Reed $\frac{60}{4}$. Picks 132. Width 22 In.

	LBS.	OZ.	AT	$	C.
8100 Ends $\frac{23}{30}$ deniers or 1¼ drams					
Organzine, Ital. Extra	18	5		90	
Tram, $\frac{14}{16}$, 6 threads					
Re-reels No. 1	19	3	80	72	20
Dyeing, pure dye	37		30	11	10
Winding, dyed weight	30		12	3	60
Quilling	15		12	1	80
Warping, 8100 ends unpicked			70	5	67
Beaming and Picking				5	67
Twisting				2	05
Weaving 280 yards			24	67	20
Picking 280 yards			2	5	60
Finishing 280 yards				5	60
Harness and Reed for Jacquard		⅙		12	
Designing, Etc., 600 cards			4	24	
General Expenses, 15 %				46	18
580 Yds. cost $				352	87
1 Yard costs net - -			$ 1	25	
Discount, Com. and Interest, 15 %			22		
85 per 100			1 47		
Addition 10 %, 90 per 100			16		
Sale Price per yard - -			$ 1	63	

Calculation of ARMURE for TIE SILK.

Warp 300 Yds.   Cloth 285 Yds.   Reed $\frac{50}{}$.   Picks 88.   Width 24 In.

	LBS.	OZ.	AT	$	c.
5920 Ends 1¼ dram					
Organzine Jap. best No. 1	12	8	4 50	56	25
Tram Jap. re-reels 4¼ drams or $\frac{12}{13}$ 5 threads	11	8	3 90	44	85
Dyeing, pure dye	24		30	7	20
Winding	19		14	2	66
Quilling	10		14	1	40
Warping 5,920 ends				2	95
Beaming and Picking				2	95
Twisting				1	50
Weaving 285 yards			10	28	50
Picking 285 yards			1	2	85
Finishing 285 yards			2	5	70
Harness and Reed for Jacquards		$\frac{1}{10}$		6	
Designing, Etc., 2 patterns				16	
General expenses, 15 %				26	82
285 yards cost $				205	63

1 yard costs net - - - - - 72
Discount, Com. and Interest, 15 %   12
                       85 per 100
                                         84
Addition 10 %, 90 per 100   9
Sale Price per yard   - $ 93

Calculation of SATIN COTTON BACK FIGURED TIE SILK. ⅓ Over.

Warp 300 Yds. Cloth 282 Yds. Reed ⁵⁄₂. Picks 88. Width 24 In.

	LBS.	OZ.	AT	$	c.
8540 Ends, 1½ dram, ¾ d.				8	
Organzine Ital. Extra	16	5	00	80	00
Tram, Canton Fil 5½ dram	5	3	30	16	50
Egypt. Cotton, ⁵⁰⁄	40		55	22	
Dyeing of Silk p. d.	21		30	6	30
Dyeing of Cotton	40		15	6	
Winding of Silk	16	14		2	24
Winding of Cotton	40	6		2	40
Quilling	45	6		2	70
Warping 8540 Ends un-picked			50	4	27
Beaming and Picking				4	27
Twisting				2	15
Weaving 282 yards			20	56	40
Picking 282 yards			2	5	64
Finishing 282 yards			4	11	28
Harness and Reed for Jacquard,		¹⁄₁₀		7	
Designing, Etc., 2 patterns in 282 yards				9	
General Expenses 15 %				43	09
282 Yds. cost				281	24
1 Yard costs net - - - -			99		
Discount, Com. and Interest 15 %			18		
85 per 100			1 17		
Addition 10 %, 90 per 100			13		
Sale Price per yard		$	1 30		

Calculation of

Warp. .....Yds. Cloth......Yds. Reed.........Picks........Width......Inch.

Organzine

Tram

Dyeing

Winding

Quilling

Warping

Beaming

Twisting

Weaving

Picking

Finishing

Harness and Reed

Designing, etc.

General Expenses

         Yards cost $

Yard costs net - - - - - - - $

Discount, Com. and Interest

Addition

Sale Price, per yard - - - - - - - $

Calculation of ....

Warp........ Yds. Cloth........ Yds. Reed........ Picks........ Width........ In.

Organzine

Tram

Dyeing

Winding

Quilling

Warping

Beaming

Twisting

Weaving

Picking

Finishing

Harness and Reed

Designing, etc.

General Expenses

                         Yards cost $

1 Yard costs net   -   -   -   -   -   - $

Discount, Com. and Interest

Addition

Sale Price, per yard   -   -   -   -   - $

Calculation of

Warp....... Yds. Cloth....... Yds. Reed........ Picks........ Width.... Inch.

Organzine

Tram

Dyeing

Winding

Quilling

Warping

Beaming

Twisting

Weaving

Picking

Finishing

Harness and Reed

Designing, etc.

General Expenses

         Yards cost $

Yard costs net - - - - - - $

Discount, Com. and Interest

Addition

Sale Price, per yard - - - - - - $

Calculation of

Warp....... Yds. Cloth...... Yds. Reed....... Picks....... Width...

Organzine

Tram

Dyeing

Winding

Quilling

Warping

Beaming

Twisting

Weaving

Picking

Finishing

Harness and Reed

Designing, etc.

General Expenses

                                                          Yards cost $

1 Yard costs net   -   -   -   -   -   - $

Discount, Com. and Interest

Addition

Sale Price, per yard   -   -   -   -   - $

Warp......Yds. Cloth......Yds. Reed......Picks......Width..........In.

Organzine

Tram

Dyeing

Winding

Quilling

Warping

Beaming

Twisting

Weaving

Picking

Finishing

Harness and Reed

Designing, etc.

General Expenses,

                          Yards cost $

1 Yard costs net - - - - - - $

Discount, Com. and Interest

Addition,

Sale Price, per yard - - - - - - $

Calculation of

Warp........ Yds. Cloth........ Yds. Reed........ Picks........ Width........ In.

Organzine

Tram

Dyeing

.

Winding

Quilling

Warping

Beaming

Twisting

Weaving

Picking

Finishing

Harness and Reed

Designing, etc.

General Expenses

                                        Yards cost $ _____

1 Yard costs net   -   -   -   -   -   - $ _____

Discount, Com. and Interest

Addition

Sale Price, per yard   -   -   -   -   - $ _____

Calculation of

Warp ..... Yds. Cloth ...... Yds. Reed ...... Picks ...... Width ......

Organzine

Tram

Dyeing

Winding

Quilling

Warping

Beaming

Twisting

Weaving

Picking

Finishing

Harness and Reed

Designing, etc.

General Expenses,

          Yards cost $

1 Yard costs net   -   -   -   -   -   - $

Discount, Com. and Interest

Addition,

Sale Price, per yard   -   -   -   -   -   - $

Calculation of

Warp...... Yds. Cloth....... Yds. Reed....... Picks........ Width....... In.

Organzine

Tram

Dyeing

Winding

Quilling

Warping

Beaming

Twisting

Weaving

Picking

Finishing

Harness and Reed

Designing, etc.

General Expenses

	Yards cost	$
1 Yard costs net - - - - - -		$
Discount, Com. and Interest		
Addition		
Sale Price, per yard - - - - -		$

Calculation of

Warp...... Yds. Cloth........ Yds. Reed........ Picks .... Width........ In.

Organzine

Tram

Dyeing

Winding

Quilling

Warping

Beaming

Twisting

Weaving

Picking

Finishing

Harness and Reed

Designing, etc.

General Expenses

                                      Yards cost $

Yard costs net - - - - - - $

Discount, Com. and Interest

Addition

Sale Price, per yard - - - - - - $

Calculation of

Warp....... Yds. Cloth....... Yds. Reed....... Picks....... Width..

Organize

Tram

Dyeing

Winding

Quilling

Warping

Beaming

Twisting

Weaving

Picking

Finishing

Harness and Reed

Designing, etc.

General Expenses

            Yards cost $ _____ _____ _____

1 Yard costs net - - $

Discount, Com. and Interest   _____ _____

Addition   _____ _____

Sale Price, per yard - - - - - $

Calculation of

Warp ..... Yds. Cloth ..... Yds. Reed ..... Picks ..... Width ..... In.

Organzine

Tram

Dyeing

Winding

Quilling

Warping

Beaming

Twisting

Weaving

Picking

Finishing

Harness and Reed

Designing, etc.

General Expenses

          Yards cost $

Yard costs net - - - - - - $

Discount, Com. and Interest

Addition

Sale Price, per yard - - - - - - $

Calculation of

Warp......Yds. Cloth   Yds. Reed......Picks...   Width......I

Organize

Tram

Dyeing

Winding

Quilling

Warping

Beaming

Twisting

Weaving

Picking

Finishing

Harness and Reed

Designing, etc.

General Expenses

                         Yards cost $ ___ ___

1 Yard costs net   -   -   - $ ___

Discount, Com. and Interest   ___ ___

Addition   ___ ___

Sale Price, per yard   - - - - - $

Calculation of ....

Warp...... Yds. Cloth...... Yds. Reed...... Picks...... Width...... In.

Organzine

Tram

Dyeing

Winding

Quilling

Warping

Beaming

Twisting

Weaving

Picking

Finishing

Harness and Reed

Designing, etc.

General Expenses,

         Yards cost $ _____

Yard costs net - - - - - $

Discount, Com. and Interest

Addition,

Sale Price, per yard - - - - - - $

Calculation of

Warp........Yds. Cloth.........Yds. Reed.........Picks........Width.

Organzine

Tram

Dyeing

Winding

Quilling

Warping

Beaming

Twisting

Weaving

Picking

Finishing

Harness and Reed

Designing, etc.

General Expenses

          Yards cost $ _____

1 Yard costs net - - - - - - $ _____

Discount, Com. and Interest

Addition

Sale Price, per yard - - - - - $ _____

Calculation of _____

Warp ..... Yds. Cloth .... Yds. Reed .... Picks .... Width .... In.

Organzine

Tram

Dyeing

Winding

Quilling

Warping

Beaming

Twisting

Weaving

Picking

Finishing

Harness and Reed

Designing, etc.

General Expenses,

          Yards cost $

1 Yard costs net   -   -   -   -   - $

Discount, Com. and Interest

Addition,

Sale Price, per yard   -   -   -   -   - $

Calculation of

Warp........ Yds. Cloth........ Yds. Reed........ Picks........ Width........ In.

Organzine

Tram

Dyeing

Winding

Quilling

Warping

Beaming

Twisting

Weaving

Picking

Finishing

Harness and Reed

Designing, etc.

General Expenses

                                    Yards cost $

1 Yard costs net - - - - - - $

Discount, Com. and Interest

Addition

Sale Price, per yard - - - - - $

Calculation of

Warp...... Yds. Cloth....... Yds. Reed....... Picks....... Width..... In.

Organzine

Tram

Dyeing

Winding

Quilling

Warping

Beaming

Twisting

Weaving

Picking

Finishing

Harness and Reed

Designing, etc.

General Expenses

Yards cost $

1 Yard costs net   -   -   -   -   -   - $

Discount, Com. and Interest

Addition

Sale Price, per yard   -   -   -   -   -   - $

Calculation of

Warp........ Yds. Cloth........ Yds. Reed........ Picks........ Width........In.

Organize

Tram

Dyeing

Winding

Quilling

Warping

Beaming

Twisting

Weaving

Picking

Finishing

Harness and Reed

Designing, etc.

General Expenses

                                    Yards cost $

1 Yard costs net - - $

Discount, Com. and Interest

Addition

Sale Price, per yard - - - - - $

Calculation of

Warp....... Yds. Cloth........ Yds. Reed........ Picks...... Width........

Organzine

Tram

Dyeing

Winding

Quilling

Warping

Beaming

Twisting

Weaving

Picking

Finishing

Harness and Reed

Designing, etc.

General Expenses

                                          Yards cost $

1 Yard costs net   -   -   -   -   -   - $

Discount, Com. and Interest

Addition

Sale Price, per yard   -   -   -   -   -   - $

Calculation of

Warp........Yds. Cloth........Yds. Reed........Picks........Width........In.

Organize

Tram

Dyeing

Winding

Quilling

Warping

Beaming

Twisting

Weaving

Picking

Finishing

Harness and Reed

Designing, etc.

General Expenses

         Yards cost $

1 Yard costs net - - $

Discount, Com. and Interest

Addition

Sale Price, per yard - - - - - $

Calculation of

Warp..... Yds. Cloth...... Yds. Reed...... Picks...... Width......... In.

Organzine

Tram

Dyeing

Winding

Quilling

Warping

Beaming

Twisting

Weaving

Picking

Finishing

Harness and Reed

Designing, etc.

General Expenses,

                             Yards cost $ _____

1 Yard costs net -   -   -   -   - $ _____

Discount, Com. and Interest

Addition,

Sale Price, per yard - - - - - - $ _____

Calculation of

Warp..........Yds. Cloth..........Yds. Reed..........Picks..........Width..........In.

Organzine

Tram

Dyeing

Winding

Quilling

Warping

Beaming

Twisting

Weaving

Picking

Finishing

Harness and Reed

Designing, etc.

General Expenses

	Yards cost	$
1 Yard costs net - - - - - -		$
Discount, Com. and Interest		
Addition		
Sale Price, per yard - - - - -		$

Calculation of

Warp...... Yds. Cloth...... Yds. Reed...... Picks...... Width......

Organzine

Tram

Dyeing

Winding

Quilling

Warping

Beaming

Twisting

Weaving

Picking

Finishing

Harness and Reed

Designing, etc.

General Expenses,

         Yards cost $

1 Yard costs net - - - - - $

Discount, **Com.** and Interest

Addition,

Sale Price, **per yard** - - - - - $

Calculation of

Warp........ Yds. Cloth........ Yds. Reed........ Picks........ Width.

Organzine

Tram

Dyeing

Winding

Quilling

Warping

Beaming

Twisting

Weaving

Picking

Finishing

Harness and Reed

Designing, etc.

General Expenses

                                                        Yards cost $

1 Yard costs net   -   -   -   -   -   - $

Discount, Com. and Interest

Addition

Sale Price, per yard   -   -   -   -   - $

Calculation of

Warp........ Yds. Cloth ....Yds. Reed........ Picks........ Width........In.

Organzine

Tram

Dyeing

Winding

Quilling

Warping

Beaming

Twisting

Weaving

Picking

Finishing

Harness and Reed

Designing, etc.

General Expenses

                                  Yards cost $

1 Yard costs net - -   - - - $

Discount, Com. and Interest

Addition

Sale Price, per yard - - - - - $

Calculation of

Warp....... Yds. Cloth....... Yds. Reed....... Picks....... Width....... In.

Organize

Tram

Dyeing

Winding

Quilling

Warping

Beaming

Twisting

Weaving

Picking

Finishing

Harness and Reed

Designing, etc.

General Expenses

                              Yards cost $ _____

1 Yard costs net - - - $

Discount, Com. and Interest

Addition

Sale Price, per yard - - - - - $

Calculation of

Warp......Yds. Cloth......Yds. Reed......Picks......Width......In.

Organzine

Tram

Dyeing

Winding

Quilling

Warping

Beaming

Twisting

Weaving

Picking

Finishing

Harness and Reed

Designing, etc.

General Expenses

                                        Yards cost $

1 Yard costs net - - - - - - $

Discount, Com. and Interest

Addition

Sale Price, per yard - - - - - - $

Calculation of

Warp........Yds. Cloth........Yds. Reed........Picks........Width........In.

Organize

Tram

Dyeing

Winding

Quilling

Warping

Beaming

Twisting

Weaving

Picking

Finishing

Harness and Reed

Designing, etc.

General Expenses

          Yards cost $ _____

1 Yard costs net - - $ _____

Discount, Com. and Interest   _____

Addition   _____

Sale Price, per yard - - - - - $ _____

Calculation of

Warp......   Yds. Cloth......   Yds. Reed....   Picks......   Width......   In.

Organzine

Tram

Dyeing

Winding

Quilling

Warping

Beaming

Twisting

Weaving

Picking

Finishing

Harness and Reed

Designing, etc.

General Expenses,

                                  Yards cost $

Yard costs net   -   -   -   -   -   - $

Discount, Com. and Interest

Addition,

Sale Price, per yard   -   -   -   -   -   - $

Calculation of

Warp....... Yds. Cloth....... Yds. Reed....... Picks....... Width.

Organzine

Tram

Dyeing

Winding

Quilling

Warping

Beaming

Twisting

Weaving

Picking

Finishing

Harness and Reed

Designing, etc.

General Expenses

                            Yards cost $ _____

1 Yard costs net - - - - - - $ _____

Discount, Com. and Interest

Addition

Sale Price, per yard - - - - - $ _____

Calculation of

Warp ....Yds. Cloth...... Yds. Reed...... Picks...... Width........ In.

Organzine

Tram

Dyeing

Winding

Quilling

Warping

Beaming

Twisting

Weaving

Picking

Finishing

Harness and Reed

Designing, etc.

General Expenses,

          Yards cost $ _____

1 Yard costs net - - - - - $ _____

Discount, Com. and Interest

Addition,

Sale Price, per yard - - - - - $

Calculation of

Warp........ Yds. Cloth........ Yds. Reed........ Picks........ Width..

Organzine

Tram

Dyeing

Winding

Quilling

Warping

Beaming

Twisting

Weaving

Picking

Finishing

Harness and Reed

Designing, etc.

General Expenses

                                    Yards cost $

1 Yard costs net   -   -   -   -   - $

Discount, Com. and Interest

Dyeing

Winding

Quilling

Warping

Beaming

Twisting

Weaving

Picking

Finishing

Harness and Reed

Designing, etc.

General Expenses

        Yards cost $

Yard costs net - - - - - $

Discount, Com. and Interest

Calculation of

Warp......... Yds. Cloth......... Yds. Reed......... Picks......... Width......... In.

Organize

Tram

Dyeing

Winding

Quilling

Warping

Beaming

Twisting

Weaving

Picking

Finishing

Harness and Reed

Designing, etc.

General Expenses

             Yards cost $

1 Yard costs net - - $

Discount, Com. and Interest

Addition

Sale Price, per yard - - - - $

Calculation of

Warp........ Yds. Cloth ......Yds. Reed........ Picks..... Width..... In.

Organzine

Tram

Dyeing

Winding

Quilling

Warping

Beaming

Twisting

Weaving

Picking

Finishing

Harness and Reed

Designing, etc.

General Expenses

                          Yards cost $

1 Yard costs net - -   - - - $

Discount, Com. and Interest

Addition

Sale Price, per yard - - - - - $

Calculation of

Warp..... Yds. Cloth ..... Yds. Reed..... Picks..... Width...... In.

Organize

Tram

Dyeing

Winding

Quilling

Warping

Beaming

Twisting

Weaving

Picking

Finishing

Harness and Reed

Designing, etc.

General Expenses

                                        Yards cost $

1 Yard costs net   -   - $

Discount, Com. and Interest

Addition

Sale Price, per yard   -   -   -   -   - $

Calculation of

Warp........Yds. Cloth.......Yds. Reed........Picks....... Width........In.

Organzine

Tram

Dyeing

Winding

Quilling

Warping

Beaming

Twisting

Weaving

Picking

Finishing

Harness and Reed

Designing, etc.

General Expenses,

         Yards cost $ _____

Yard costs net - - - - - - $ _____

Discount, Com. and Interest _____

Addition, _____

Sale Price, per yard - - - - - - - $

Calculation of

Warp........ Yds. Cloth........ Yds. Reed........ Picks........ Width.

Organzine

Tram

Dyeing

Winding

Quilling

Warping

Beaming

Twisting

Weaving

Picking

Finishing

Harness and Reed

Designing, etc.

General Expenses

           Yards cost $

1 Yard costs net   -   -   -   -   -   - $

Discount, Com. and Interest

Calculation of

Warp....... Yds. Cloth...... Yds. Reed...... Picks...... Width........In.

Organzine

Tram

Dyeing

Winding

Quilling

Warping

Beaming

Twisting

Weaving

Picking

Finishing

Harness and Reed

Designing, etc.

General Expenses,

                                      Yards cost $ _____

1 Yard costs net   -   -   -   -   -   - $ _____

Discount, Com. and Interest

Addition,

Sale Price. per yard   -   -   -   -   -   - $ _____

Calculation of

Warp........Yds. Cloth........Yds. Reed........Picks........Width........In.

Organzine

Tram

Dyeing

Winding

Quilling

Warping

Beaming

Twisting

Weaving

Picking

Finishing

Harness and Reed

Designing, etc.

General Expenses

Yards cost $ _____

1 Yard costs net   -   -   -   -   -   - $

Discount, Com. and Interest

Addition

Sale Price, per yard   -   -   -   -   - $

Calculation of ....

Warp. ...... Yds. Cloth ...... Yds. Reed ...... Picks ...... Width ...... In.

Organzine

Tram

Dyeing

Winding

Quilling

Warping

Beaming

Twisting

Weaving

Picking

Finishing

Harness and Reed

Designing, etc.

General Expenses

                                        Yards cost $

1 Yard costs net - -   - - - - $

Discount, Com. and Interest

Addition

Sale Price, per yard - - - - - - $

Calculation of

Warp......Yds. Cloth......Yds. Reed......Picks......Width......In.

Organize

Tram

Dyeing

Winding

Quilling

Warping

Beaming

Twisting

Weaving

Picking

Finishing

Harness and Reed

Designing, etc.

General Expenses

                                      Yards cost $ _____

1 Yard costs net   -   - $ _____

Discount, Com. and Interest

Addition

Sale Price, per yard   -   -   -   -   - $ _____

Calculation of ....

Warp .... Yds. Cloth .... Yds. Reed .... Picks .... Width .... In.

Organzine

Tram

Dyeing

Winding

Quilling

Warping

Beaming

Twisting

Weaving

Picking

Finishing

Harness and Reed

Designing, etc.

General Expenses

                                                Yards cost $

1 Yard costs net   - - - - - - - $

Discount, Com. and Interest

Addition

Sale Price, per yard   - - - - - - - $

Calculation of

Warp...... Yds. Cloth...... Yds. Reed...... Picks...... Width...... In.

Organize

Tram

Dyeing

Winding

Quilling

Warping

Beaming

Twisting

Weaving

Picking

Finishing

Harness and Reed

Designing, etc.

General Expenses

                                 Yards cost $

1 Yard costs net - -   - $

Discount, Com. and Interest

Addition

Sale Price, per yard - - - - - $

Calculation of

Warp.. ....Yds. Cloth...... Yds. Reed.... Picks....... Width......... In.

Organzine

Tram

Dyeing

Winding

Quilling

Warping

Beaming

Twisting

Weaving

Picking

Finishing

Harness and Reed

Designing, etc.

General Expenses,

          Yards cost $ _____

= Yard costs net - - - - - - $ _____

Discount, Com. and Interest

Calculation of

Warp........ Yds. Cloth........ Yds. Reed........ Picks........ Width.

Organzine

Tram

Dyeing

Winding

Quilling

Warping

Beaming

Twisting

Weaving

Picking

Finishing

Harness and Reed

Designing, etc.

General Expenses

                                Yards cost $

1 Yard costs net   -   -   -   -   -   - $

Discount, Com. and Interest

Addition

Sale Price, per yard   -   -   -   -   - $

Calculation of

Warp......Yds. Cloth......Yds. Reed......Picks......Width......In.

Organzine

Tram

Dyeing

Winding

Quilling

Warping

Beaming

Twisting

Weaving

Picking

Finishing

Harness and Reed

Designing, etc.

General Expenses,

         Yards cost $ _____

1 **Yard costs net** - - - - - - $ _____

Discount, Com. and Interest

Addition,

Sale Price, per yard - - - - - - $ _____

Calculation of

Warp........ Yds. Cloth........ Yds. Reed........ Picks........ Width........ In.

Organzine

Tram

Dyeing

Winding

Quilling

Warping

Beaming

Twisting

Weaving

Picking

Finishing

Harness and Reed

Designing, etc.

General Expenses

          Yards cost $

1 Yard costs net - - - - - - $

Discount, Com. and Interest

Addition

Sale Price, per yard - - - - - $

Calculation of

Warp .... Yds. Cloth ..... Yds. Reed .... Picks .... Width... ...In.

Organzine

Tram

Dyeing

Winding

Quilling

Warping

Beaming

Twisting

Weaving

Picking

Finishing

Harness and Reed

Designing, etc.

General Expenses

                                  Yards cost $

1 Yard costs net -   -   -   -   -   -   - $

Discount, Com. and Interest

Addition

Sale Price, per yard -   -   -   -   -   -   - $

Calculation of

Warp....... Yds. Cloth....... Yds. Reed....... Picks....... Width ....In.

Organize

Tram

Dyeing

Winding

Quilling

Warping

Beaming

Twisting

Weaving

Picking

Finishing

Harness and Reed

Designing, etc.

General Expenses

                              Yards cost $

1 Yard costs net -   - $

Discount, Com. and Interest

Addition

Sale Price, per yard - - - - - $

Calculation of

Warp............ Yds. Cloth.............Yds. Reed............ Picks............ Width............ In.

Organzine

Tram

Dyeing

Winding

Quilling

Warping

Beaming

Twisting

Weaving

Picking

Finishing

Harness and Reed

Designing, etc.

General Expenses

                                                Yards cost $

1 Yard costs net - - -   - - - $

Discount, Com. and Interest

Addition

Sale Price, per yard - - - - - - $

Calculation of

Warp...... Yds. Cloth...... Yds. Reed...... Picks.   Width .... In.

Organize

Tram

Dyeing

Winding

Quilling

Warping

Beaming

Twisting

Weaving

Picking

Finishing

Harness and Reed

Designing, etc.

General Expenses

                                    Yards cost $

1 Yard costs net   -   -   - $

Discount, Com. and Interest

Addition

Sale Price, per yard   -   -   -   -   -   - $

Calculation of

Warp........ Yds. Cloth........ Yds. Reed...... Picks....... Width........ In.

Organzine

Tram

Dyeing

Winding

Quilling

Warping

Beaming

Twisting

Weaving

Picking

Finishing

Harness and Reed

Designing, etc.

General Expenses,

                        Yards cost $ ____

1 Yard costs net   -   -   -   -   -   - $ ____

Discount, Com. and Interest

Addition,

Sale Price, per yard   -   -   -   -   -   - $

Calculation of

Warp........ Yds. Cloth........ Yds. Reed........ Picks........ Width........ In.

Organzine

Tram

Dyeing

Winding

Quilling

Warping

Beaming

Twisting

Weaving

Picking

Finishing

Harness and Reed

Designing, etc.

General Expenses

                                        Yards cost $

1 Yard costs net   -   -   -   -   -   - $

Discount, Com. and Interest

Addition

Sale Price, per yard   -   -   -   -   - $

Calculation of

Warp	Yds. Cloth	Yds. Reed	Picks	Width	In.
Organzine					
Tram					
Dyeing					
Winding					
Quilling					
Warping					
Beaming					
Twisting					
Weaving					
Picking					
Finishing					
Harness and Reed					
Designing, etc.					
General Expenses,					

Yards cost $ _____

1 Yard costs net - - - - - - $

Discount, Com. and Interest

Addition,

Sale Price. per yard - - - - - - $

Calculation of

Warp....... Yds. Cloth....... Yds. Reed....... Picks... Width.

Organzine

Tram

Dyeing

Winding

Quilling

Warping

Beaming

Twisting

Weaving

Picking

Finishing

Harness and Reed

Designing, etc.

General Expenses

          Yards cost $ _____

1 Yard costs net - - - - - $ _____

Discount, Com. and Interest

Addition

Sale Price, per yard - - - - - $ _____

Calculation of

Warp...... Yds. Cloth...... ...Yds. Reed........ Picks...... .... Width........ . In.

Organzine

Tram

Dyeing

Winding

Quilling

Warping

Beaming

Twisting

Weaving

Picking

Finishing

Harness and Reed

Designing, etc.

General Expenses

                                            Yards cost $

1 Yard costs net - -   - - - - $

Discount, Com. and Interest

Addition

Sale Price, per yard - - - - - - - $

Calculation of

Warp......Yds. Cloth   Yds. Reed...   Picks.   Width.....In.

Organize

Tram

Dyeing

Winding

Quilling

Warping

Beaming

Twisting

Weaving

Picking

Finishing

Harness and Reed

Designing, etc.

General Expenses

                              Yards cost $ _____ _____

1 Yard costs net   -   -   - $ _____

Discount, Com. and Interest   _____ _____

Addition   _____ _____

Calculation of

Warp...... Yds. Cloth .....Yds. Reed ...... Picks. . Width. .... In.

Organzine

Tram

Dyeing

Winding

Quilling

Warping

Beaming

Twisting

Weaving

Picking

Finishing

Harness and Reed

Designing, etc.

General Expenses

         Yards cost $

1 Yard costs net - - - - - - $

Discount, Com. and Interest

Addition

Sale Price, per yard - - - - - - $

Calculation of

Warp ...... Yds. Cloth .... Yds. Reed .... Picks .... Width .....

Organize

Tram

Dyeing

Winding

Quilling

Warping

Beaming

Twisting

Weaving

Picking

Finishing

Harness and Reed

Designing, etc.

General Expenses

            Yards cost $ ___

1 Yard costs net - -   - $ ___

Discount, Com. and Interest   ___

Addition   ___

Sale Price, per yard - - - - - - $

Calculation of

Warp......Yds. Cloth......Yds. Reed......Picks......Width........In.

Organzine

Tram

Dyeing

Winding

Quilling

Warping

Beaming

Twisting

Weaving

Picking

Finishing

Harness and Reed

Designing, etc.

General Expenses,

                              Yards cost $ _____

1 Yard costs net   -   -   -   -   -   - $ _____

Discount, Com. and Interest

Addition.

Calculation of

Warp. .... Yds. Cloth. ...... Yds. Reed. ...... Picks. ...... Width..

Organzine

Tram

Dyeing

Winding

Quilling

Warping

Beaming

Twisting

Weaving

Picking

Finishing

Harness and Reed

Designing, etc.

General Expenses

         Yards cost $

1 Yard costs net - - - - - $

Discount, Com. and Interest

Addition

Sale Price, per yard - - - - - $

Calculation of..........

Warp.......Yds. Cloth......Yds. Reed......Picks......Width........In.

Organzine

Tram

Dyeing

Winding

Quilling

Warping

Beaming

Twisting

Weaving

Picking

Finishing

Harness and Reed

Designing, etc.

General Expenses,

                                    Yards cost $

1 Yard costs net   -   -   -   -   -   - $

Discount, Com. and Interest

Addition,

Sale Price, per yard   -   -   -   -   -   - $

Calculation of

Warp......... Yds. Cloth......... Yds. Reed......... Picks......... Width.

Organzine

Tram

Dyeing

Winding

Quilling

Warping

Beaming

Twisting

Weaving

Picking

Finishing

Harness and Reed

Designing, etc.

General Expenses

                                        Yards cost $ _____

1 Yard costs net - - - - - - $ _____

Discount, Com. and Interest

Addition

Sale Price, per yard - - - - - $ _____

Calculation of

Warp........ Yds. Cloth........ Yds. Reed........ Picks........ Width........ In.

Organzine

Tram

Dyeing

Winding

Quilling

Warping

Beaming

Twisting

Weaving

Picking

Finishing

Harness and Reed

Designing, etc.

General Expenses

                                        Yards cost $

1 Yard costs net - -   - - - - $

Discount, Com. and Interest

Addition

Sale Price, per yard - - - - - - $

Calculation of

Warp......Yds. Cloth......Yds. Reed......Picks......Width......In.

Organize

Tram

Dyeing

Winding

Quilling

Warping

Beaming

Twisting

Weaving

Picking

Finishing

Harness and Reed

Designing, etc.

General Expenses

        Yards cost $ _____

1 Yard costs net - -   - $ _____

Discount, Com. and Interest

Addition

Sale Price, per yard - - - - - $

Calculation of ....

Warp........ Yds. Cloth .... Yds. Reed .... Picks........ Width.. .... In.

Organzine

Tram

Dyeing

Winding

Quilling

Warping

Beaming

Twisting

Weaving

Picking

Finishing

Harness and Reed

Designing, etc.

General Expenses

            Yards cost $

1 Yard costs net   -   -   -   -   -   - $

Discount, Com. and Interest

Addition

Sale Price, per yard   -   -   -   -   -   - $

Calculation of

Warp...... Yds. Cloth...... Yds. Reed....... Picks...... Width...... In.

Organize

Tram

Dyeing

Winding

Quilling

Warping

Beaming

Twisting

Weaving

Picking

Finishing

Harness and Reed

Designing, etc.

General Expenses

          Yards cost $ _____

1 Yard costs net - - $

Discount, Com. and Interest

Addition

Sale Price, per yard - - - - - $

Calculation of

Warp........ Yds. Cloth........ Yds. Reed........ Picks........ Width........ In.

Organzine

Tram

Dyeing

Winding

Quilling

Warping

Beaming

Twisting

Weaving

Picking

Finishing

Harness and Reed

Designing, etc.

General Expenses,

         Yards cost $

1 Yard costs net   -   -   -   -   - $

Discount, Com. and Interest

Addition,

Sale Price, per yard   -   -   -   -   - $

Calculation of

Warp. ..... Yds. Cloth........ Yds. Reed......... Picks......... Width. .... In.

Organzine

Tram

Dyeing

Winding

Quilling

Warping

Beaming

Twisting

Weaving

Picking

Finishing

Harness and Reed

Designing, etc.

General Expenses

            Yards cost $ _____

1 Yard costs net - - - - - - $ _____

Discount, Com. and Interest

Addition

Sale Price, per yard - - - - - $ _____

Calculation of

Warp...... Yds. Cloth...... Yds. Reed...... Picks...... Width...... In.

Organzine

Tram

Dyeing

Winding

Quilling

Warping

Beaming

Twisting

Weaving

Picking

Finishing

Harness and Reed

Designing, etc.

General Expenses,

Yards cost $

1 Yard costs net -   -   -   -   - $

Discount, Com. and Interest

Addition,

Sale Price, per yard -   -   -   -   - $

Calculation of

Warp........Yds. Cloth........Yds. Reed........Picks........Width........In.

Organzine

Tram

Dyeing

Winding

Quilling

Warping

Beaming

Twisting

Weaving

Picking

Finishing

Harness and Reed

Designing, etc.

General Expenses

Yards cost $

1 Yard costs net   -   -   -   -   -   - $

Discount, Com. and Interest

Addition

Sale Price, per yard   -   -   -   -   - $

Calculation of

Warp...... Yds. Cloth ...... Yds. Reed ...... Picks ...... Width....

Organzine

Tram

Dyeing

Winding

Quilling

Warping

Beaming

Twisting

Weaving

Picking

Finishing

Harness and Reed

Designing, etc.

General Expenses

                                      Yards cost $

1 Yard costs net - -   - - - $

Discount, Com. and Interest

Addition

Calculation of

Warp........ Yds. Cloth....... Yds. Reed....... Picks........ Width........ In.

Organize

Train

Dyeing

Winding

Quilling

Warping

Beaming

Twisting

Weaving

Picking

Finishing

Harness and Reed

Designing, etc.

General Expenses

          Yards cost $

1 Yard costs net - - $

Discount, Com. and Interest

Addition

Sale Price, per yard - - - - - $

Calculation of

Warp...... Yds. Cloth ...... Yds. Reed ...... Picks ...... Width ...... In=

Organzine

Tram

Dyeing

Winding

Quilling

Warping

Beaming

Twisting

Weaving

Picking

Finishing

Harness and Reed

Designing, etc.

General Expenses

        Yards cost $

1 Yard costs net - - - - - $

Discount, Com. and Interest

Addition

Sale Price, per yard - - - - - $

Calculation of

Warp....... Yds. Cloth .... Yds. Reed ...... Picks.   Width ..... In.

Organize

Tram

Dyeing

Winding

Quilling

Warping

Beaming

Twisting

Weaving

Picking

Finishing

Harness and Reed

Designing, etc.

General Expenses

                               Yards cost $ _____

1 Yard costs net   -   -   - $

Discount, Com. and Interest

Addition

Sale Price, per yard   -   -   -   -   - $

WARP WEIGHT TABLES.

LENGTH: 100 YDS.

WEIGHT TABLE

For the Use of Raw Silk, in a Warp of 100 Yards.

No. of Ends.	DENIERS.								
	10/12	12/14	14/16	16/18	18/20	20/22	22/24	24/26	28/30
	DRAMS.								
	5/8	3/4	7/8	1	1 1/4	1 1/4	1 3/8	1 1/2	1 3/4
	POUNDS, OUNCES AND DRAMS.								
1000	4¹	4¹⁴	5¹¹	6⁸	7⁵	8²	8¹⁵	9¹²	11⁶
1200	4¹⁴	5¹⁴	6¹³	7¹³	8¹²	9¹²	10¹²	11¹¹	13¹⁰
1400	5¹¹	6⁴	7¹⁵	9²	10¹	11⁶	12⁸	13¹⁰	15¹⁵
1600	6⁸	7¹³	9²	10⁶	11¹¹	13—	14⁵	15¹⁰	1.2⁸
1800	7⁵	8¹²	10⁴	11¹¹	13⁵	15¹⁴	1.0¹	1.1⁹	1.4⁸
2000	8²	9¹²	11⁶	13—	14¹⁰	1.0⁴	1.1¹¹	1.3⁸	1.6¹²
2200	8¹⁵	10¹²	12⁸	14⁵	1.0¹	1.1¹¹	1.3¹¹	1.5⁷	1.9
2400	9¹²	11¹¹	13¹⁰	15¹⁰	1.1⁹	1.3⁸	1.5⁷	1.7⁶	1.11⁵
2600	10⁹	12¹²	14¹³	1.0¹⁴	1.3	1.5²	1.8¹	1.9⁶	2.13⁵
2800	10¹⁵	13²	15⁶	1.1⁶	1.3¹¹	1.5¹⁴	1.8¹	1.10⁴	1.14¹⁰
3000	12³	14¹⁰	1.1¹	1.3⁸	1.5¹⁵	1.8⁶	1.10¹³	1.13⁴	2.2²
3200	13—	15¹⁰	1.2³	1.4¹³	1.7⁶	1.10	1.12¹⁰	1.15⁵	2.4⁶
3400	13¹³	1.0⁹	1.3⁵	1.6²	1.8¹⁴	1.11¹⁰	1.14⁶	2.1²	2.6¹¹
3600	14¹⁰	1.1⁹	1.4⁸	1.7⁶	1.10⁵	1.13⁴	2.0³	2.3²	2.8¹⁵
3800	15⁷	1.2⁸	1.5¹⁰	1.8¹¹	1.11¹²	1.14¹⁴	2.1¹⁵	2.5¹	2.11⁴
4000	1.0⁴	1.3⁸	1.6¹²	1.10	1.13⁴	2.0⁸	2.3¹²	2.7	2.13¹⁰
4200	1.1¹	1.4⁸	1.7¹⁴	1.11⁵	1.14¹¹	2.2²	2.5⁹	2.8¹⁵	2.15¹²
4400	1.1¹⁴	1.5⁷	1.9	1.12¹⁰	2.0⁵	2.3¹²	2.7⁵	2.10¹¹	3.2¹
4600	1.2¹¹	1.6⁷	1.10⁵	1.13¹⁴	2.1¹⁰	2.5⁶	2.9²	2.12¹¹	3.4⁵
4800	1.3⁸	1.7⁶	1.11⁵	1.15³	2.3²	2.7	2.10¹¹	2.14¹³	3.6¹⁰
5000	1.4⁵	1.8⁶	1.12⁷	2.0⁸	2.4⁹	2.8¹⁰	2.12¹¹	3.0¹²	3.8¹⁴
5200	1.5²	1.9⁶	1.13⁹	2.1¹³	2.6	2.10⁴	2.14⁸	3.2¹¹	3.11²
5400	1.5¹⁵	1.10⁵	1.14¹¹	2.3²	2.7⁸	2.11¹⁴	3.0⁴	3.4¹⁰	3.13⁵
5600	1.6¹²	1.11⁵	1.15¹⁴	2.4⁶	2.8¹⁵	2.13⁸	3.2¹	3.6¹⁰	3.15¹¹
5800	1.7⁹	1.12⁴	2.1	2.5¹¹	2.10⁷	2.15²	3.3³	3.8⁹	4.2
6000	1.8⁶	1.13⁴	2.2²	2.7	2.11¹⁴	3.0¹²	3.5¹⁰	3.10⁸	4.4⁴
6200	1.9³	1.14⁴	2.3⁴	2.8⁵	2.13⁵	3.2⁶	3.7⁷	3.12⁷	4.6⁸
6400	1.10	1.15³	2.4⁶	2.9¹⁰	2.14¹³	3.4	3.9³	3.14⁶	4.8¹³
6600	1.10¹³	2.0³	2.5⁹	2.10¹⁴	3.0⁴	3.5¹⁰	3.11	4.0⁶	4.11¹
6800	1.11¹⁰	2.1²	2.6¹¹	2.12³	3.1¹²	3.7⁴	3.12¹²	4.2⁵	4.13⁶
7000	1.12⁷	2.2²	2.7¹³	2.13⁸	3.3³	3.8¹⁴	3.14⁹	4.4¹	4.15¹⁰
7200	1.13⁴	2.3²	2.8⁵	2.14¹³	3.4¹⁰	3.10⁸	4.0⁶	4.6³	5.1¹⁴
7400	1.14¹	2.4¹	2.10¹	3.0²	3.6²	3.12²	4.2²	4.8²	5.4³
7600	1.14¹⁴	2.5¹	2.11¹⁴	3.1⁶	3.7⁹	3.13¹²	4.3¹⁵	4.10²	5.6⁷
7800	1.15¹¹	2.6	2.12⁶	3.3	3.9¹	3.15⁶	4.5¹¹	4.12¹	5.8¹²
8000	2.0⁸	2.7	2.13⁸	3.4	3.10⁸	4.1	4.7⁹	4.14	5.11

Above weights include 4 per cent. for waste.

LENGTH: 100 YDS.

WEIGHT TABLE

For the Use of Raw Silk, in a Warp of 100 Yards.

No. of Ends	\(\frac{30}{32}\)	\(\frac{32}{34}\)	\(\frac{36}{38}\)	\(\frac{40}{42}\)	\(\frac{42}{44}\)	\(\frac{44}{46}\)	\(\frac{46}{48}\)	\(\frac{50}{52}\)	\(\frac{56}{60}\)
	1¾	2	2⅛	2⅜	2½	2⅝	2¾	3	3½
	DENIERS — DRAMS — POUNDS, OUNCES AND DRAMS								
1000	12³	13	13¹³	15⁷	1.0⁴	1.1¹	1.1¹⁴	1.3⁸	1.6¹²
1200	14¹⁰	15¹⁰	1.0⁹	1.2⁸	1.3⁸	1.4⁸	1.5⁷	1.7⁶	1.11⁴
1400	1.1¹	1.2³	1.3⁵	1.5¹⁰	1.6¹²	1.8⁸	1.9	1.11⁶	1.15¹⁴
1600	1.3⁸	1.4¹³	1.6²	1.8¹¹	1.10	1.11⁵	1.12¹⁰	1.15³	2.4⁶
1800	1.5¹⁵	1.7⁶	1.8¹⁴	1.11¹³	1.13⁴	1.14¹¹	2.0³	2.3²	2.5
2000	1.8⁶	1.10	1.11¹⁰	1.14¹⁴	2.0⁸	2.2²	2.3¹²	2.7	2.7⁸
2200	1.10¹³	1.12¹⁰	1.14⁶	2.1¹⁵	2.3¹²	2.5⁹	2.7⁵	2.10¹⁴	3.2
2400	1.13¹	1.15³	2.1²	2.5¹	2.7	2.8¹⁵	2.10¹⁴	2.14¹³	3.6¹⁰
2600	1.15¹¹	2.1¹³	2.3¹⁵	2.8⁷	2.10⁴	2.12⁶	2.14⁶	3.2¹¹	3.7²
2800	2.0¹³	2.3	2.5³	2.9⁹	2.11¹²	2.13¹⁵	3.0²	3.4⁸	3.13⁴
3000	2.4⁹	2.7	2.9⁷	2.14⁵	3.0¹²	3.3	3.5¹⁰	3.10⁸	4.4⁴
3200	2.7	2.9¹⁰	2.12³	3.1⁶	3.4	3.6¹⁰	3.9³	3.14⁶	4.8¹²
3400	2.9⁷	2.12³	2.14¹⁵	3.4⁸	3.7⁴	3.10	3.12¹²	4.2⁵	4.13⁶
3600	2.11¹¹	2.14¹³	3.1¹²	3.7³	3.10⁸	3.13⁷	4.0⁶	4.6³	5.1¹⁴
3800	2.14⁵	3.1⁶	3.4⁸	3.10¹¹	3.13¹²	4.0¹³	4.3¹⁵	4.10²	5.6⁸
4000	3.0¹²	3.4	3.7⁴	3.13¹²	4.1	4.4⁴	4.7⁸	4.14	5.7
4200	3.3³	3.6¹⁰	3.10	4.0¹³	4.4⁸	4.7¹¹	4.11¹	5.1¹⁴	5.15⁸
4400	3.5¹⁰	3.9³	3.12¹²	4.3¹⁵	4.7⁸	4.11¹	4.14¹⁰	5.5¹³	6.4²
4600	3.7⁷	3.11¹³	3.15⁹	4.7	4.10¹²	4.14⁸	5.2⁴	5.9¹¹	6.8¹⁰
4800	3.10⁸	3.14⁷	4.2⁵	4.8⁴	4.14	5.1¹⁴	5.5¹³	5.13¹⁰	6.13⁴
5000	3.12¹⁵	4.1	4.5¹	4.13³	5.1⁸	5.5⁵	5.9⁶	6.1⁸	7.1¹²
5200	3.15⁶	4.3¹¹	4.7¹³	5.0⁴	5.4⁸	5.8¹²	5.12¹⁵	6.5⁶	7.6⁴
5400	4.1¹³	4.6³	4.10⁹	5.3⁸	5.7¹²	5.12²	6.0⁸	6.9⁶	7.10¹⁴
5600	4.4⁴	4.8¹³	4.13⁶	5.6⁷	5.11	5.15⁹	6.4²	6.13³	7.15⁶
5800	4.6¹¹	4.11⁶	5.0²	5.9¹⁰	5.14⁸	6.2¹⁵	6.7¹¹	7.1²	8.4
6000	4.9²	4.14	5.2¹⁴	5.12¹⁰	6.1⁸	6.6⁶	6.11⁴	7.5	8.8⁸
6200	4.11⁹	5.0¹⁰	5.5¹⁰	5.15¹¹	6.4¹²	6.9¹³	6.14¹³	7.8¹⁴	8.13
6400	4.14	5.3³	5.8⁶	6.2¹³	6.8	6.13³	7.2⁸	7.12¹³	9.1¹⁰
6600	5.0⁷	5.5¹³	5.11¹³	6.5¹⁴	6.11⁴	7.0¹⁰	7.6	8.0¹¹	9.6⁷
6800	5.2¹⁴	5.8⁶	5.13¹⁵	6.9	6.14⁸	7.4	7.9⁹	8.4¹⁰	9.10¹²
7000	5.5⁵	5.11	6.0¹¹	6.12¹	7.1¹²	7.7⁷	7.13²	8.8⁸	9.15⁴
7200	5.7¹²	5.13¹⁰	6.3⁷	6.15⁴	7.5¹⁰	7.10¹⁴	8.0¹¹	8.12⁶	10.3¹²
7400	5.10³	6.0³	6.6³	7.2¹	7.8⁴	7.14⁴	8.4⁴	9.0⁵	10.8⁶
7600	5.13⁴	6.2¹³	6.9	7.5¹⁵	7.11⁸	8.1¹¹	8.7¹⁴	9.4³	10.12¹⁴
7800	5.15¹	6.5⁶	6.11¹²	7.8⁷	7.14¹²	8.5¹	8.11⁷	9.8²	11.1⁸
8000	6.1⁸	6.8	6.14⁸	7.11⁸	8.2	8.8⁸	8.15	9.12	11.6

Above weights include 4 per cent. for waste.

LENGTH: 100 YDS.

WEIGHT TABLE

FOR THE USE OF RAW SILK, IN A WARP OF 100 YARDS.

No. of Ends.	DENIERS.								
	$\frac{10}{12}$	$\frac{12}{14}$	$\frac{14}{16}$	$\frac{16}{18}$	$\frac{18}{20}$	$\frac{20}{22}$	$\frac{22}{24}$	$\frac{24}{26}$	$\frac{28}{30}$
	DRAMS.								
	$\frac{5}{8}$	$\frac{3}{4}$	$\frac{7}{8}$	1	$1\frac{1}{8}$	$1\frac{1}{4}$	$1\frac{3}{8}$	$1\frac{1}{2}$	$1\frac{3}{4}$
	POUNDS, OUNCES AND DRAMS.								
8200	2.1^5	2.8	2.14^{10}	3.5^5	3.11^{15}	4.2^{10}	4.9^5	4.15^{15}	5.13^4
8400	2.2^2	2.8^{15}	2.15^{12}	3.6^{10}	3.13^6	4.4^4	4.11^1	5.1^{14}	5.15^9
8600	2.2^{15}	2.9^{15}	3.0^{15}	3.7^{14}	3.14^{14}	4.5^{14}	4.12^{14}	5.3^{14}	6.1^{13}
8800	2.3^{12}	2.10^{14}	3.2^1	3.9^3	4.0^6	4.7^8	4.14^{10}	5.5^{13}	6.4^2
9000	2.4^9	2.11^{14}	3.3^3	3.10^8	4.2^{13}	4.9^2	5.0^7	5.7^{12}	6.6^6
9200	2.5^6	2.12^{14}	3.4^5	3.11^{13}	4.3^4	4.10^{14}	5.2^4	5.9^{11}	6.8^{10}
9400	2.6^3	2.13^{13}	3.5^7	3.13^2	4.4^{15}	4.12^6	5.4	5.11^{10}	6.10^{15}
9600	2.7	2.14^{13}	3.6^{10}	3.14^6	4.6^3	4.14	5.5^{13}	5.13^{10}	6.13^3
9800	2.7^{13}	2.15^{12}	3.7^{12}	3.15^{11}	4.7^{11}	4.15^{10}	5.7^9	5.15^9	7.0^2
10000	2.8^{10}	3.0^{12}	3.8^{14}	4.1	4.9^2	5.1^4	5.9^6	6.1^8	7.1^{12}
10200	2.9^7	3.1^{12}	3.10	4.2^5	4.10^9	5.2^{14}	5.11^3	6.3^7	7.4
10400	2.10^4	3.2^{11}	3.11^2	4.3^{10}	4.12^1	5.4^8	5.12^{15}	6.5^6	7.6^5
10600	2.11^1	3.3^{11}	3.12^5	4.4^{14}	4.13^8	5.6^2	5.14^{12}	6.7^6	7.8^9
10800	2.11^{14}	3.4^{12}	3.13^7	4.6^3	4.15	5.7^{12}	6.0^8	6.9^5	7.10^{15}
11000	2.12^{11}	3.5^{10}	3.14^9	4.7^8	5.0^7	5.9^6	6.2^5	6.11^{14}	7.13^2
11200	2.13^8	3.6^{10}	3.15^{11}	4.8^{13}	5.1^{14}	5.11	6.4^2	6.13^3	7.15^3
11400	2.14^5	3.7^9	4.0^{13}	4.10^2	5.3^6	5.12^{10}	6.5^{14}	6.15^2	8.1^{11}
11600	2.15^2	3.8^9	4.2	4.11^6	5.4^{13}	5.14^4	6.7^{11}	7.1^2	8.3^{15}
11800	2.15^{15}	3.9^8	4.3^2	4.12^{11}	5.6^5	5.15^{14}	6.9^7	7.3^1	8.6^{14}
12000	3.0^{12}	3.10^8	4.4^4	4.14	5.7^{12}	6.1^8	6.11^4	7.5	8.8^8
12200	3.1^9	3.11^6	4.5^6	4.15^5	5.9^3	6.3^2	6.13^1	7.6^{15}	8.10^{12}
12400	3.2^6	3.12^7	4.6^8	5.0^{10}	5.10^{11}	6.4^{12}	6.11^{13}	7.8^{14}	8.13^1
12600	3.3^3	3.13^7	4.7^{11}	5.1^{14}	5.12^2	6.6^6	7.0^{10}	7.10^{14}	8.15^5
12800	3.4	3.14^6	4.8^{13}	5.3^3	5.13^{10}	6.8	7.2^6	7.12^{13}	9.1^{10}
13000	3.4^{13}	3.15^6	4.9^{15}	5.4^9	5.15^1	6.9^{10}	7.4^3	7.14^{12}	9.3^{14}
13200	3.5^{10}	4.0^6	4.11^1	5.5^{13}	6.0^8	6.11^4	7.6	8.0^{11}	9.6^2
13400	3.6^7	4.1^5	4.12^3	5.7^2	6.2	6.12^{14}	7.7^{12}	8.2^{10}	9.8^7
13600	3.7^4	4.2^5	4.13^6	5.8^6	6.3^7	6.14^8	7.9^9	8.4^{10}	9.10^{11}
13800	3.8^1	4.3^4	4.14^8	5.9^{11}	6.4^{15}	7.0^2	7.11^5	8.6^9	9.13
14000	3.8^{14}	4.4^4	4.15^{10}	5.11	6.6^6	7.1^{12}	7.13^2	8.8^8	9.15^4
14200	3.9^{11}	4.5^4	5.0^{12}	5.12^5	6.7^{13}	7.3^6	7.14^{15}	8.10^7	10.1^8
14400	3.10^8	4.6^3	5.1^{14}	5.13^{10}	6.9^5	7.5	8.0^{11}	8.12^6	10.3^{13}
14600	3.11^5	4.7^3	5.3^1	5.14^{14}	6.10^{13}	7.6^{10}	8.2^8	8.14^6	10.6^1
14800	3.12^2	4.8^2	5.4^3	6.0^3	6.12^4	7.8^1	8.4^4	9.0^5	10.8^6
15000	3.12^{15}	4.9^2	5.5^5	6.1^8	6.13^{11}	7.9^{14}	8.6^1	9.2^4	10.10^{10}

Above weights include 4 per cent. for waste.

LENGTH: 100 YDS.

WEIGHT TABLE

For the Use of Raw Silk, in a Warp of 100 Yards.

No. of Ends	DENIERS								
	$\frac{3\,2}{3\,2}$	$\frac{3\,2}{3\,4}$	$\frac{3\,6}{3\,8}$	$\frac{1\,0}{1\,2}$	$\frac{1\,2}{1\,4}$	$\frac{1\,4}{1\,6}$	$\frac{1\,6}{1\,8}$	$\frac{2\,0}{2\,2}$	$\frac{2\,6}{2\,8}$
	DRAMS.								
	$1\frac{7}{8}$	2	$2\frac{1}{8}$	$2\frac{1}{4}$	$2\frac{1}{2}$	$2\frac{5}{8}$	$2\frac{3}{4}$	3	$3\frac{1}{2}$
	POUNDS, OUNCES AND DRAMS.								
8200	6.3¹⁵	6.10¹⁰	7.1⁴	7.14⁹	8.5⁴	8.11¹⁵	9.2⁹	9.15¹⁴	11.10⁸
8400	6.6⁶	6.13³	7.4	8.11¹	8.8⁸	8.15³	9.6²	10.3¹³	11.15²
8600	6.8¹³	6.15¹³	7.6¹³	8.4¹²	8.11¹²	9.2¹⁷	9.9¹²	10.7¹¹	12.3¹⁰
8800	6.11⁴	7.2⁶	7.9⁹	8.7¹⁴	8.15	9.6²	9.13⁵	10.11¹⁶	12.8⁴
9000	6.13¹¹	7.5	7.12⁵	8.10¹³	9.2⁴	9.9⁹	10.0¹⁴	10.15⁶	12.12¹²
9200	7.0²	7.7¹⁰	7.15¹	8.14	9.5⁸	9.13	10.4⁷	11.3⁶	13.1⁴
9400	7.2⁹	7.10³	8.1¹³	9.1²	9.8¹²	10.0⁶	10.8	11.7⁵	13.5¹⁴
9600	7.5	7.12¹³	8.4¹⁰	9.4³	9.12	10.3¹³	10.10²	11.11³	13.10⁶
9800	7.7⁷	7.15⁶	8.7⁶	9.7⁵	9.15⁴	10.7³	10.15³	11.15²	14.0⁴
10000	7.9¹⁴	8.2	8.10²	9.10⁶	10.2⁸	10.10¹⁰	11.2¹²	12.3	14.3⁸
10200	7.12⁵	8.4¹⁰	8.12¹⁴	9.13⁷	10.5¹²	10.14¹	11.6⁵	12.6¹⁵	14.8
10400	7.14¹²	8.7²	8.15¹⁰	10.0⁹	10.9	11.1⁷	11.9¹⁴	12.10¹³	14.12¹⁰
10600	8.1³	8.9¹³	9.2⁷	10.3¹⁰	10.12⁴	11.4¹⁴	11.13⁸	12.14¹¹	15.1²
10800	8.3¹⁰	8.12⁶	9.5³	10.6¹²	10.15⁸	11.8⁴	12.1¹	13.2¹⁰	15.5¹²
11000	8.6¹	8.15	9.7¹³	10.9¹³	11.2¹²	11.11¹¹	12.4,⁹	13.6⁸	15.10⁴
11200	8.8⁸	9.1¹⁰	9.10¹¹	10.12¹⁴	11.6	12.0¹	12.8²	13.10⁶	15.14¹²
11400	8.10¹⁵	9.4⁷	9.13⁷	11.00	11.9¹⁴	12.2⁸	12.11¹²	13.14⁵	16.3¹²
11600	8.13⁶	9.6¹³	10.0⁴	11.3¹	11.12⁸	12.5¹³	12.15⁶	14.2⁹	16.7¹⁴
11800	8.15¹³	9.9⁶	10.3	11.6⁵	11.15¹²	12.9⁵	13.2¹⁵	14.6²	16.13¹²
12000	9.2⁴	9.12	10.5¹²	11.9⁴	12.3	12.12¹⁷	13.6⁸	14.10	17.1
12200	9.4¹¹	9.14¹⁰	10.8⁸	11.12⁵	12.6⁴	13.0⁸	13.10¹	14.13¹⁴	17.5⁸
12400	9.7²	10.1³	10.11¹	11.15⁷	12.9⁸	13.3⁹	13.13¹⁰	15.1¹²	17.10²
12600	9.9⁹	10.3³	10.14¹	12.2⁸	12.12¹⁷	13.7	14.1⁴	15.5¹¹	17.14¹⁰
12800	9.12	10.6⁶	11.0¹⁵	12.5¹⁰	13.—	13.10⁶	14.4³	15.9¹⁰	18.3⁴
13000	9.14⁷	10.9	11.3⁹	12.8¹¹	13.3⁴	13.13¹³	14.8⁶	15.13⁹	18.7¹²
13200	10.0¹⁴	10.11¹⁰	11.6⁵	12.11¹²	13.6⁸	14.1⁴	14.11¹⁵	16.1⁶	18.12⁴
13400	10.3⁵	10.14³⁰	11.9¹	12.14¹⁴	13.9¹²	14.4¹⁰	14.15⁸	16.5⁶	19.0¹⁴
13600	10.5¹²	11.0¹³	11.11¹⁴	13.1¹⁵	13.13	14.8¹	15.3²	16.9³	19.5⁶
13800	10.8³	11.3⁶	11.14¹⁰	13.5¹	14.0⁴	14.11⁷	15.6¹¹	16.13²	19.10
14000	10.10¹⁰	11.6	12.1⁶	13.8²	14.3⁸	14.14¹⁴	15.10⁴	17.1	19.14⁶
14200	10.13¹	11.8¹⁰	12.4²	13.11³	14.6¹²	15.2⁵	15.13¹³	17.4¹⁴	20.3
14400	10.15⁸	11.11³	12.6¹⁴	13.14⁵	14.10	15.5¹¹	16.1⁶	17.8¹³	20.7¹⁰
14600	11.1¹⁵	11.13¹³	12.9¹	14.1⁶	14.13⁴	15.9³	16.5	17.12¹¹	20.12²
14800	11.4⁶	12.0⁶	12.12⁷	14.4⁸	15.0⁸	15.12⁸	16.8⁹	18.0¹⁰	21.0¹¹
15000	11.6¹³	12.3	12.15³	14.7⁹	15.3¹²	15.15¹⁵	16.12²	18.4⁸	21.5⁴

Above weights include 4 per cent. for waste.

LENGTH: 300 YDS.

WEIGHT TABLE

FOR THE USE OF RAW SILK, IN A WARP OF 300 YARDS.

No. of Ends.	DENIERS.								
	$\frac{10}{12}$	$\frac{12}{14}$	$\frac{14}{16}$	$\frac{16}{18}$	$\frac{18}{20}$	$\frac{20}{22}$	$\frac{22}{24}$	$\frac{24}{26}$	$\frac{26}{28}$
	DRAMS.								
	$\frac{5}{8}$	$\frac{3}{4}$	$\frac{7}{8}$	1	$1\frac{1}{8}$	$1\frac{1}{4}$	$1\frac{3}{8}$	$1\frac{1}{2}$	$1\frac{3}{4}$
	POUNDS, OUNCES AND DRAMS.								
1000	12³	14¹⁰	1.1¹	1.3⁸	1 5¹⁵	1.8⁶	1.10¹⁵	1.13⁴	2.2²
1200	14¹⁰	1.1⁸	1.4⁷	1.7⁶	1.10⁵	1 13⁴	2.0²	2.3¹	2 8¹⁵
1400	1.1¹	1.4⁷	1.7¹⁴	1.11⁴	1.14¹¹	2 2²	2.5⁸	2.8¹⁵	2.15¹²
1600	1.3⁹	1.7⁶	1.11⁴	1.15³	2.3¹	2 7	2.10¹⁴	2.14¹²	3.6⁹
1800	1.5¹⁵	1.10⁵	1.14¹¹	2.3¹	2.7⁷	2.11¹⁴	3.0⁴	3.4¹⁰	3.13⁶
2000	1.8⁶	1 13⁴	2.2²	2.7	2.11¹⁴	3.0¹²	3.5¹⁰	3.10⁸	4.4⁴
2200	1.10¹⁵	2.0²	2.5⁹	2.10¹⁴	3.0⁴	3.5¹⁰	3.10¹⁵	4 0⁵	4.11¹
2400	1.13⁴	2.3¹	2.8¹⁵	2.14¹²	3.4¹⁰	3.10⁸	1 0⁵	4.6⁹	5.1¹⁴
2600	1.15¹¹	2.6⁹	2.12⁵	3.2¹⁴	3.9	3.15⁶	4.5¹¹	4.12	5.8¹¹
2800	2.2²	2 8¹⁵	2.15¹²	3 6⁹	3.13⁶	4 4⁴	4.11¹	5.1¹⁴	5.15⁸
3000	2.4⁹	2.11¹⁴	3 3³	3.10⁸	4.1¹³	4.9²	5.0⁷	5.7¹²	6 6⁶
3200	2.7	2.14¹²	3.6⁹	3.14⁶	4.6³	4.14	5.5¹²	5.13⁹	6.13³
3400	2.9⁷	3.1¹¹	3.10	4.2⁴	4.10⁹	5 2¹⁴	5.11²	6.3⁷	7.4
3600	2.11¹⁴	3.4¹⁰	3 13⁶	4.6³	4.14¹⁵	5.7¹²	6.0⁸	6.9¹	7.10¹³
3800	2.14⁵	3 7⁹	4.0¹⁵	4.10¹	5.3⁵	5.12¹⁰	6.5¹⁴	6 15²	8.1¹⁰
4000	3.0¹²	3.10⁸	4.4⁴	4.14	5.7¹²	6.1⁸	6.11⁴	7.5	8 8⁸
4200	3.3³	3.13⁶	4.7¹⁰	5.1¹⁴	5.12²	6.6⁶	7.0⁹	7.10¹³	8.15⁵
4400	3.5¹⁰	4.0⁵	1.11	5.5¹²	6.0⁸	6.11⁴	7.5¹⁵	8.0¹¹	9.6²
4600	3.8¹	4 3³	4.14⁷	5 9¹⁰	6.4¹⁴	7.0²	7.11⁴	8 6⁸	9.12¹⁵
4800	3.10⁸	4.6²	5 1⁴	5.13⁸	6.9⁴	7.5	8 0¹⁰	8.12⁶	10.3¹²
5000	3.12¹⁵	4.9²	5.5	6.1⁸	6.13¹¹	7.9¹⁴	8.6¹	9.2⁴	10.10¹⁰
5200	3.15⁶	4.12	5.8¹¹	6.5⁶	7.2¹	7.14¹²	8.11⁶	9 8¹	11.1⁷
5400	4.1¹³	4.14¹⁵	5.12²	6.9⁴	7.6⁷	8.3¹⁰	9 0¹²	9.13¹⁵	11.8⁴
5600	4 4⁴	5.1¹⁴	5.15⁸	6.13⁹	7.10¹³	8.8⁸	9.6²	10.3¹²	11.15¹
5800	4.6¹¹	5.4¹³	6.2¹⁵	7.1¹	7.15³	8.13⁶	9.11⁷	10.9¹⁰	12.5¹⁴
6000	4.9²	5.7¹²	6 6⁶	7.5	8.3¹⁰	9.2⁴	10.0¹⁴	10.15⁸	12.12¹²
6200	4.11⁹	5.10¹⁰	6.9¹²	7.8¹⁴	8.8	9.7²	10.6³	11.5⁵	13.3⁹
6400	4.14	5.13⁹	6.13³	7.12¹²	8.12⁶	9.12	10.11⁹	11.11²	13.10⁶
6600	5.0⁷	6.0⁷	7.0⁹	8.0¹⁰	9.0¹²	10.0¹⁴	11.0¹⁴	12.1	14.1³
6800	5.2¹⁴	6.3⁶	7.4	8.4⁹	9 5²	10.5¹²	11.6¹	12.6¹³	14.8
7000	5.5⁵	6.6⁵	7.7⁷	8.8⁸	9.9⁹	10.10¹⁰	11.11¹¹	12.12¹²	14.14¹⁴
7200	5.7¹²	6.9⁴	7.10¹³	8.12⁶	9.13¹⁵	10.15⁸	12.1	13.2⁹	15.5¹¹
7400	5.10³	6.12³	7.14⁴	9.0⁴	10.2⁵	11.4⁶	12.6⁶	13.8⁷	15.12⁸
7600	5.12¹⁰	6.15²	8.1¹⁰	9.4⁹	10.6¹¹	11.9⁴	12.11¹²	13.14¹	16.3⁵
7800	5.15¹	7.2¹	8.5¹	9 8¹	10.11¹	11.14²	13.1²	14.4²	16.10²
8000	6.1⁸	7.5	8.8⁸	9.12	10.15⁸	12.3	13.6⁹	14.10	17.1

Above weights include 4 per cent. for waste.

LENGTH: 300 YDS.

WEIGHT TABLE

For the Use of Raw Silk, in a Warp of 300 Yards.

No. of Ends.	DENIERS								
	30/32	32/34	36/38	40/42	42/44	44/46	46/48	50/52	56/58
	DRAMS								
	$1\frac{7}{8}$	2	$2\frac{1}{8}$	$2\frac{3}{8}$	$2\frac{1}{2}$	$2\frac{5}{8}$	$2\frac{3}{4}$	3	$3\frac{1}{4}$
	POUNDS, OUNCES AND DRAMS								
1000	2.4^{9}	2.7^{0}	2.9^{7}	2.14^{5}	3.0^{12}	3.3^{2}	3.5^{10}	3.10^{3}	4.4^{4}
1200	2.11^{14}	2.14^{12}	3.1^{11}	3.7^{9}	3.10^{6}	3.13^{6}	4.0^{5}	4.6^{3}	5.1^{14}
1400	3.3^{3}	3.6^{9}	3.10	4.0^{13}	4.4^{1}	4.7^{10}	4.11^{1}	5.1^{14}	5.15^{6}
1600	3.10^{8}	3.14^{7}	4.2^{4}	4.10^{1}	4.14	5.1^{14}	5.5^{12}	5.13^{9}	6.13^{2}
1800	4.1^{13}	4.6^{3}	4.10^{9}	5.3^{5}	5.7^{12}	5.12^{2}	6.0^{8}	6.9^{4}	7.10^{12}
2000	4.9^{2}	4.14	5.2^{14}	5.12^{10}	6.1^{8}	6.6^{6}	6.11^{4}	7.5	8.8^{8}
2200	5.0^{7}	5.5^{12}	5.11^{2}	6.5^{14}	6.11^{4}	7.0^{9}	7.5^{15}	8.0^{11}	9.5^{2}
2400	5.7^{12}	5.13^{9}	6.3^{7}	6.15^{2}	7.5^{0}	7.10^{13}	8.0^{11}	8.12^{6}	10.3^{12}
2600	5.15^{1}	6.5^{6}	6.11^{11}	7.8^{5}	7.14^{12}	8.5^{1}	8.11^{6}	9.8^{1}	11.1^{6}
2800	6.6^{6}	6.13^{3}	7.4	8.1^{10}	8.8^{8}	8.15^{5}	9.6^{2}	10.3^{12}	11.15
3000	6.13^{11}	7.5^{0}	7.12^{5}	8.10^{15}	9.2^{4}	9.9^{9}	10.0^{14}	10.15^{8}	12.12^{12}
3200	7.5	7.12^{12}	8.4^{9}	9.4^{3}	9.12	10.3^{12}	10.11^{9}	11.11^{3}	13.10^{6}
3400	7.12^{5}	8.4^{9}	8.12^{14}	9.13^{7}	10.5^{12}	10.14	11.6^{5}	12.6^{14}	14.8
3600	8.3^{10}	8.12^{6}	9.5^{2}	10.6^{11}	10.15^{8}	11.8^{4}	12.1	13.2^{9}	15.5^{10}
3800	8.11	9.4^{3}	9.13^{7}	10.15^{15}	11.9^{4}	12.2^{8}	12.11^{12}	13.14^{4}	16.3^{4}
4000	9.2^{4}	9.12	10.5^{12}	11.9^{4}	12.3	12.12^{12}	13.6^{8}	14.10	17.1
4200	9.9^{9}	10.3^{12}	10.14	12.2^{8}	12.12^{12}	13.6^{15}	14.1^{3}	15.5^{11}	17.14^{10}
4400	10.0^{14}	10.11^{9}	11.6^{5}	12.11^{12}	13.6^{8}	14.1^{3}	14.11^{14}	16.1^{6}	18.12^{4}
4600	10.8^{3}	11.3^{5}	11.14^{9}	13.5	14.0^{4}	14.11^{6}	15.6^{10}	16.13^{1}	19.9^{14}
4800	10.15^{8}	11.11^{2}	12.6^{14}	13.14^{4}	14.10	15.5^{10}	16.1^{6}	17.8^{12}	20.7^{8}
5000	11.6^{13}	12.3	12.15^{3}	14.7^{9}	15.3^{12}	15.15^{15}	16.12^{2}	18.4^{6}	21.5^{4}
5200	11.14^{2}	12.10^{12}	13.7^{7}	15.0^{13}	15.13^{8}	16.10^{2}	17.6^{13}	19.0^{3}	22.2^{14}
5400	12.5^{7}	13.2^{9}	13.15^{12}	15.10^{1}	16.7^{4}	17.4^{6}	18.1^{9}	19.11^{14}	23.0^{8}
5600	12.12^{12}	13.10^{6}	14.8	16.3^{5}	17.1	17.14^{10}	18.12^{4}	20.7^{9}	23.14^{2}
5800	13.4^{1}	14.2^{3}	15.0^{5}	16.12^{9}	17.10^{12}	18.8^{14}	19.7	21.3^{4}	24.4^{12}
6000	13.11^{6}	14.10	15.8^{10}	17.5^{14}	18.4^{8}	19.3^{2}	20.1^{12}	21.15	25.9^{8}
6200	14.2^{11}	15.1^{12}	16.0^{14}	17.15^{2}	18.14^{4}	19.13^{5}	20.12^{7}	22.10^{11}	26.7^{2}
6400	14.10	15.9^{8}	16.9^{3}	18.8^{6}	19.8	20.7^{9}	21.7^{2}	23.6^{6}	27.4^{12}
6600	15.1^{5}	16.1^{6}	17.1^{7}	19.1^{10}	20.1^{12}	21.1^{13}	22.1^{14}	24.2^{1}	28.2^{6}
6800	15.8^{10}	16.9^{2}	17.9^{11}	19.10^{14}	20.11^{8}	21.12	22.12^{10}	24.13^{12}	$29.-$
7000	15.15^{15}	17.1	18.2^{1}	20.4^{3}	21.5^{4}	22.6^{5}	23.7^{6}	25.9^{0}	29.13^{12}
7200	16.7^{4}	17.8^{12}	18.10^{3}	20.13^{7}	21.15	23.0^{8}	24.2^{5}	26.5^{3}	30.11^{6}
7400	16.14^{9}	18.0^{9}	19.2^{10}	21.6^{11}	22.8^{12}	23.10^{12}	24.12^{12}	27.0^{14}	31.9
7600	17.5^{14}	18.8^{6}	19.10^{14}	21.15^{15}	23.2^{8}	24.5	25.7^{9}	27.12^{9}	32.6^{10}
7800	17.13^{3}	19.0^{3}	20.3^{3}	22.9^{3}	23.12^{4}	24.15^{4}	26.2^{4}	28.8^{4}	33.4^{4}
8000	18.4^{8}	19.8	20.11^{8}	23.2^{8}	24.6	25.9^{8}	26.13	29.4	34.2

Above weights include 4 per cent. for waste.

Length: 300 Yds.

Weight Table

For the Use of Raw Silk, for a Warp of 300 Yards.

No. of Ends.	DENIERS								
	$\frac{12}{13}$	$\frac{13}{14}$	$\frac{14}{15}$	$\frac{15}{16}$	$\frac{18}{20}$	$\frac{20}{22}$	$\frac{22}{24}$	$\frac{24}{26}$	$\frac{26}{28}$
	DRAMS								
	$\frac{5}{8}$	$\frac{3}{4}$	$\frac{7}{8}$	1	$1\frac{1}{8}$	$1\frac{1}{4}$	$1\frac{3}{8}$	$1\frac{1}{2}$	$1\frac{3}{4}$
	POUNDS, OUNCES AND DRAMS								
8200	6.3¹⁵	7.7¹⁴	8.11¹⁴	9.15¹⁴	11.3¹⁴	12.7¹⁴	13.11¹³	14.15¹³	17 7¹³
8400	6.6⁶	7.10¹³	8.15⁵	10.3¹²	11.8⁴	12.12¹²	14.1³	15.5¹¹	17.14¹⁰
8600	6.8¹³	7.13¹¹	9 2¹¹	10.7¹¹	11.12¹⁰	13.1¹⁰	14.6⁹	15.11⁰	18.5⁷
8800	6.11⁴	8.0¹¹	9.6	10.11⁹	12.1	13.6⁶	14.11¹⁵	16.1⁶	18.12⁴
9000	6.13¹¹	8 3¹⁰	9.9⁹	10.15⁸	12.5⁷	13.11⁶	15.1⁵	16.7⁴	19.3²
9200	7.0²	8.6⁹	9.12¹⁵	11.3⁶	12.9¹⁵	14.0⁴	15.6¹⁰	16.13¹	19.9¹⁵
9400	7.2⁹	8.9⁷	10.0⁶	11.7⁴	12.14³	14.5²	15.12	17 2¹⁵	20.0¹²
9600	7.5	8.12⁶	10.3¹²	11.11³	13.2¹⁰	14.10	16.1⁶	17.8¹²	20.7⁹
9800	7.7⁷	8.15⁵	10.7³	11.15¹	13.7	14.14¹⁴	16.6¹¹	17.14¹⁰	20.14⁶
10000	7.9¹⁴	9.2⁴	10.10¹⁰	12.3	13.11⁶	15.3¹²	16.12²	18.4⁸	21.5⁴
10200	7.12⁵	9.5²	10.14	12.6¹⁴	13.15¹²	15.8¹⁰	17.17	18.10⁵	21 12¹
10400	7.14¹²	9.8	11.1⁶	12.10¹²	14.4²	15.13⁸	17.6¹²	19.0²	22.2¹⁴
10600	8.1³	9.10¹⁵	11.4¹³	12.14¹⁰	14.8⁸	16.2⁶	17.12²	19.6	22.9¹¹
10800	8.3¹⁰	9.13¹⁴	11.8⁴	13.2⁸	14.12¹⁴	16.7⁴	18.1⁸	19.11¹⁴	23.0⁸
11000	8.6¹	10.0¹³	11.11¹⁰	13.6⁷	15.1⁴	16.12²	18.6¹⁴	20.1¹¹	23.7⁵
11200	8.8⁸	10.3¹²	11.15	13.10⁶	15.5¹⁰	17.1	18.12⁴	20.7⁸	23 14²
11400	8.10¹⁵	10.6¹¹	12.2⁷	13.14⁴	15.10	17.5¹⁴	19.1⁹	20.13⁶	24.4¹⁵
11600	8.13⁶	10.9¹⁰	12.5¹⁴	14.2²	15.14⁶	17.10¹²	19.6¹⁴	21.3⁴	24.11¹²
11800	8.15¹³	10.12⁹	12.9⁵	14.6¹	16.2¹²	17.15¹⁰	19.12⁵	21.9²	25.2¹⁰
12000	9.2⁴	10.15⁸	12.12¹²	14.10	16.7⁴	18.4⁸	20.1²	21.15	25.9⁸
12200	9.4¹¹	11.2⁶	13.0²	14.13¹⁴	16.11¹⁰	18.9⁶	20.7¹	22.4³	26.0⁵
12400	9.7²	11.5⁴	13.3⁸	15.1¹²	17.0	18.14⁴	20.12⁶	22.10¹⁰	26.7²
12600	9.9⁹	11.8³	13.6¹⁵	15.5¹⁰	17.4⁶	19.3²	21.1¹²	23.0⁷	26.13¹⁵
12800	9.12	11.11²	13.10⁶	15.9⁸	17.8¹²	19.8	21.7⁸	23.6⁴	27.4¹²
13000	9.14⁷	11.14	13.13¹²	15.13⁶	17.13²	19.13¹⁵	21.12⁷	23.12³	27.11⁹
13200	10.0¹⁴	12.0¹⁴	14.1²	16.1⁴	18.1⁸	20.1¹²	22.1¹²	24.2	28.2⁶
13400	10.3⁵	12.4¹³	14.4⁹	16.5³	18.5¹⁴	20.6¹⁰	22.7²	24.7¹³	28.9³
13600	10.5¹²	12.6¹²	14.8	16.9²	18.10⁴	20.11⁸	22.12⁸	24.13¹⁰	29.-
13800	10.8³	12.9¹²	14.11⁷	16.13¹	18.14¹¹	21.0⁶	23.1¹⁵	25.3⁹	29.6¹⁴
14000	10.10¹⁰	12.12¹²	14.14¹⁴	17.1	19 3²	21.5⁴	23.7⁶	25.9⁸	29.13¹²
14200	10.13¹	13.15¹⁰	15.2⁴	17.4¹⁴	19.7⁸	21.10²	23.12¹¹	25.15⁵	30.4⁹
14400	10.15⁸	13.2⁸	15.5¹⁰	17.9¹²	19.11¹⁴	21.15	34.2	26.5²	30.11⁶
14600	11.1¹⁵	13.5⁷	15.9¹	17.12¹⁰	20.0⁴	22.3¹⁴	24.7⁶	26.11	31.2⁸
14800	11.4⁶	13.8⁶	15.12⁸	18.0⁸	20.4¹⁰	22.8¹²	24.12	27.0¹¹	31.9
15000	11.6¹³	13.11⁵	15.15¹⁴	18.4⁷	20.9	22.13¹⁰	25.2⁷	27.6¹¹	31.15¹³

Above weights include 4 per cent. for waste

LENGTH: 300 YDS.

WEIGHT TABLE

For the Use of Raw Silk, in a **WARP** of 300 Yards.

No. of Ends.	DENIERS.							
	$\frac{30}{32}$	$\frac{32}{34}$	$\frac{36}{38}$	$\frac{40}{42}$	$\frac{42}{44}$	$\frac{44}{46}$	$\frac{46}{48}$	$\frac{50}{52}$
	DRAMS.							
	$1\frac{7}{8}$	2	$2\frac{1}{8}$	$2\frac{1}{4}$	$2\frac{3}{8}$	$2\frac{1}{2}$	$2\frac{5}{8}$	$2\frac{3}{4}$
	POUNDS, OUNCES AND DRAMS.							
8200	18.11[13]	19.15[12]	21.3[12]	23.11[12]	24.15[12]	26.3[11]	27.7[11]	29.15[11]
8400	19.3[2]	20.7[9]	21.12[1]	24.5	25.9[8]	26.13[15]	28.2[7]	30.11[6]
8600	19.10[7]	20.15[6]	22.4[5]	26.6[4]	26.3[4]	27.8[3]	28.13[2]	31.7[1]
8800	20.1[12]	21.7[2]	22.12[10]	25.7[8]	26.13	28.2[7]	29.7[14]	32.2[12]
9000	20.9[1]	21.15	23.4[15]	26.0[13]	27.6[12]	28.12[11]	30.2[10]	32.14[8]
9200	21.0[6]	22.6[12]	23.13[2]	26.10[1]	28.0[8]	29.6[14]	30.13[6]	33.10[3]
9400	21.7[11]	22.14[9]	24.5[8]	27.3[5]	28.10[4]	30.1[2]	31.8[2]	34.5[14]
9600	21.15	23.6[6]	24.13[12]	27.12[9]	29.4	30.11[5]	32.2[13]	35.1[9]
9800	22.6[5]	23.14[3]	25.6	28.5[13]	29.13[12]	31.5[10]	32.13[8]	35.13[4]
10000	22.13[10]	24.6	25.14[8]	28.15[2]	30.7[8]	31.15[14]	33.8[4]	36.9
10200	23.4[15]	24.13[12]	26.6[10]	29.8[6]	31.1[4]	32.10[1]	34.2[15]	37.4[11]
10400	23.12[4]	25.5[8]	26.14[14]	30.1[10]	31.11	33.4[4]	34.13[10]	38.0[6]
10600	24.3[9]	25.13[5]	27.7[3]	30.10[14]	32.4[12]	33.14[0]	35.8[6]	38.12[1]
10800	24.10[14]	26.5[2]	27.15[8]	31.4[3]	32.14[8]	34.8[12]	36.3[2]	39.7[12]
11000	25.2[3]	26.12[15]	28.7[12]	31.13[6]	33.8[4]	35.3	36.13[13]	40.3[8]
11200	25.9[8]	27.4[12]	29.--	32.6[10]	34.2	35.13[4]	37.8[0]	40.15[3]
11400	26.0[13]	27.12[9]	29.8[5]	32.15[14]	34.11[12]	36.7[8]	38.3[4]	41.10[14]
11600	26.8[2]	28.4[6]	30.0[10]	33.9[2]	35.5[8]	37.1[12]	38.14	42.6[9]
11800	26.15[7]	28.12[4]	30.8[15]	34.2[7]	35.15[4]	37.12	39.8[12]	43.2[4]
12000	27.7[12]	29.4	31.1[8]	34.11[12]	36.9	38.6[4]	40.3[8]	43.14
12200	27.14[1]	29.11[12]	31.9[8]	35.5	37.2[12]	39.0[7]	40.14[3]	44.9[11]
12400	28.5[6]	30.3[8]	32.1[12]	35.14[4]	37.12[8]	39.10[10]	41.8[14]	45.5[6]
12600	28.12[11]	30.11[4]	32.10[1]	36.7[9]	38.6[4]	40.4[14]	42.3[9]	46.1[1]
12800	29.4	31.3	33.2[6]	37.0[12]	39.--	40.15[2]	42.14[4]	46.12[12]
13000	29.11[5]	31.10[14]	33.10[10]	37.10	39.9[12]	41.9[5]	43.9	47.8[8]
13200	30.2[10]	32.2[12]	34.2[14]	38.3[4]	40.3[8]	42.3[8]	44.3[12]	48.4[2]
13400	30.9[15]	32.10[8]	34.11[2]	38.12[8]	40.13[4]	42.13[12]	44.14[8]	48.15[14]
13600	31.1[4]	33.2[1]	35.3[6]	39.5[12]	41.7	43.8	45.9[4]	49.11[6]
13800	31.8[9]	33.10[2]	35.11[12]	39.15[1]	42.0[12]	44.2[5]	46.4	50.6[4]
14000	31.15[14]	34.2	36.4[2]	40.8[6]	42.10[8]	44.12[10]	46.14[12]	51.3
14200	32.7[3]	34.10[12]	36.12[4]	41.1[10]	43.4[4]	45.6[13]	47.9[7]	51.14[11]
14400	32.14[8]	35.1[8]	37.4[6]	41.10[14]	43.14	46.1	48.4[2]	52.10[6]
14600	33.5[13]	35.9[3]	37.12[13]	42.4[2]	44.7[12]	46.11[4]	48.14[13]	53.6[1]
14800	33.13[2]	36.1[2]	38.5[4]	42.13[6]	45.1[8]	47.5[8]	49.9[8]	54.1[12]
15000	34.4[7]	36.8[15]	38.13[9]	43.6[10]	45.11[4]	47.15[12]	50.4[4]	54.13[6]

Above weights include 4 per cent. for waste.

LENGTH: 100 YDS.

WEIGHT TABLE
OF COTTON OR SPUN SILK YARNS, FOR A WARP OF 100 YARDS.

No. of Ends.	DRAMS.							
	15	12	10	9½	7½	6¾	6	5¾
	YARNS 2-PLY.—ENGL. NUMBERS.							
	40	50	60	70	80	90	100	110
	POUNDS, OUNCES AND DRAMS.							
1000	6.3	4.15	4.2	3.9	3.2	2.12	**2.8**	2.4
1200	7.10[10]	5.15	4.15[4]	4.4[5]	3.11[7]	3.4[13]	**2.15[8]**	2.11[5]
1400	8.10[10]	6.15	5.13[9]	4.15[2]	4.5	3.13[10]	**3.7[7]**	3.2[6]
1600	9.14[7]	7.14[11]	6.9[7]	5.10[8]	4.15[4]	4.6[6]	**3.15[6]**	3.11[11]
1800	11.2[5]	8.14[10]	7.6[14]	6.5[13]	5.6[14]	4.15[4]	**4.7[5]**	4.1
2000	12.6[2]	9.14[7]	8.4[1]	7.1[4]	6.3	5.8	**4.15[5]**	4.8
2200	13.10	10.15	9.2	7.13	6.13	6.1	**5.7**	4.15
2400	14.13[11]	11.14[10]	9.15	8.8	7.7	6.9	**5.15**	4.6[7]
2600	16.1[8]	12.14	10.11[7]	9.4	8.1	7.2	**6.5**	5.14
2800	17.5[5]	13.13[13]	11.8[14]	9.14[7]	8.10[10]	7.11[6]	**6.14[11]**	6.5
3000	18.9[2]	14.13[11]	12.6[1]	10.9[13]	9.4[9]	8.4[1]	**7.6[14]**	6.11[11]
3200	19.13	15.5[4]	13.3[5]	11.5[2]	9.14[7]	8.13	**7.14[14]**	7.3[4]
3400	21.0[13]	16.6[10]	14.0[6]	12.0[7]	10.8[6]	9.5[9]	**8.7**	7.10[7]
3600	22.4[9]	17.13[4]	14.13[11]	13.0[10]	11.2[4]	9.11[7]	**8.14[10]**	8.1[11]
3800	23.8[6]	18.13[2]	15.10[15]	13.7[1]	11.12[3]	10.7[4]	**9.6[8]**	8.8[14]
4000	24.12[3]	19.12[13]	16.8[2]	14.2[6]	12.6[1]	11.0[3]	**9.14[7]**	9.0[1]
4200	26.—	20.12[12]	17.5[5]	14.13[11]	13.—	11.8[14]	**10.6[6]**	9.7[4]
4400	....	21.11[14]	18.2[8]	15.9[3]	13.9[14]	12.1[7]	**10.14[5]**	9.14[7]
4600	....	22.12[8]	18.15[13]	16.4[6]	14.3[12]	12.10[12]	**11.6[4]**	10.5[9]
4800	....	....	19.13	16.15[13]	14.15[8]	13.3[5]	**11.15[4]**	10.12[14]
5000	....	....	20.10[2]	18.0[7]	15.7[13]	13.12[2]	**12.6[1]**	11.4
5200	....	....	....	18.6[6]	16.1[8]	14.4[13]	**12.14**	11.11[6]
5400	....	....	....	19.1[10]	16.11[7]	14.13[6]	**13.5[14]**	12.2[8]
5500	....	....	....	....	17.0[6]	15.2[4]	**13.9[13]**	12.6[1]
5600	....	....	....	....	17.10[2]	15.6[9]	**13.13[14]**	12.9[11]
5800	....	....	....	....	....	15.15[3]	**14.5[12]**	13.0[14]
6000	....	....	....	....	....	16.8[2]	**14.13[11]**	13.8[7]
6200	....	....	....	....	....	....	**15.5[10]**	13.15[6]
6400	....	....	....	....	....	....	**15.13[10]**	14.6[8]
6600	....	....	....	....	....	....	....	14.13[11]
6800	....	....	....	....	....	....	....	15.5[8]

Above table is figured for 2-ply yarns and includes 4 per cent. for waste.

Sizes are in English numbers and paralleled in drams; **Spun Silk Yarns, however, have half the numbers of drams and half the weight their numbers indicate, i. e.: for a warp of 4,000 ends we have to figure the weight for a Spun Silk Warp as** 2,000 ends.

LENGTH: 100 YDS.

WEIGHT TABLE

OF COTTON OR SPUN SILK YARNS, FOR A WARP OF 100 YARDS.

No. of Ends.	DRAMS.							
	5	$4\frac{3}{4}$	$4\frac{1}{2}$	$3\frac{3}{4}$	$3\frac{1}{2}$	3	$2\frac{3}{4}$	$2\frac{1}{2}$
	YARNS 2-PLY. ENGL. NUMBERS.							
	120	130	140	160	180	200	220	240
	POUNDS, OUNCES AND DRAMS.							
1000	2.1	1.15	1.12	1.9	1.6	1.4	1.2	1.1
1200	2.7^9	2.4^9	2.2	1.13^{11}	1.10^9	1.8	1.5	1.13^{13}
1400	2.11^3	2.10^{12}	2.7^9	2.2^{10}	1.14^{12}	1.11^{11}	1.9^4	1.7^2
1600	3.4^{15}	3.1	2.13^6	2.7^{13}	2.3^3	1.15^6	1.12^{13}	1.10^7
1800	3.11^{10}	3.6^{12}	3.2^{15}	2.12^5	2.7^{10}	2.3^9	2.0	1.13^{11}
2000	4.—	3.13^3	3.8^{10}	3.1^7	2.12	2.7^{10}	2.4	2.1
2200	4.9	4.3	3.14	3.7	3	2.12	2.8	2.4
2400	4.15^3	4.9^2	4.4	3.11^7	3.5	2.15^9	2.11^3	2.7^{10}
2600	5.5^{11}	4.15^3	4.9^{11}	4.0^{10}	3.10	3.3^9	2.14^{12}	2.10^{11}
2800	5.12^7	5.5^5	4.15^4	4.5^3	3.13^{10}	3.7^7	3.2^8	2.14^9
3000	6.3^1	5.11^7	5.5	4.10^1	4.2	3.11^7	3.6	3.1^8
3200	6.9^{10}	6.1^8	5.10^7	4.15^1	4.6^7	3.15^6	3.9^{10}	3.4^{12}
3400	7.0^3	6.7^{11}	6.0^4	5.4^3	4.10^{12}	4.3^5	3.13^1	3.8
3600	7.6^{11}	6.13^{11}	6.5^{15}	5.9^2	4.15^1	4.75	4.0^{15}	3.11^7
3800	8.0^{14}	7.3^8	6.12	5.14	5.3^2	4.10^{10}	4.47	3.14^{11}
4000	8.4^6	7.9^{13}	7.1^3	6.3	5.8	4.15^4	4.8	4.2
4200	8.10^{10}	8.—	7.6^{14}	6.8	5.12^7	5.3^3	4.11^{10}	4.5^3
4400	9.1^{14}	8.6^2	7.11^7	6.12^{11}	6.0^{13}	5.7^2	4.14^{12}	4.8^9
4600	9.8	8.12^4	8.2^3	7.1^{15}	6.5^4	5.11^2	5.2^{14}	4.11^{14}
4800	9.14^8	9.2^2	8.7^{13}	7.6^9	6.9^3	5.15^4	5.6^7	4.15^4
5000	10.5^1	9.8^6	8.13^9	7.11^{12}	6.14^7	6.3^1	5.10	5.2^9
5200	10.11^8	9.14^9	9.3^3	8.1	7.2^6	6.7	5.13^{10}	5.5^{13}
5400	11.2^4	10.4^{10}	9.8^{13}	8.5^1	7.6^9	6.11^1	6.1^4	5.9^2
5500	11.5^6	10.7^{11}	9.11^9	8.8^1	7.9^4	6.13	6.3^4	5.10^{13}
5600	11.8^{13}	10.10^{10}	9.14^8	8.10^{10}	7.10^2	6.14^{15}	6.4^{12}	5.12^7
5800	11.15^2	11.0^{12}	10.4^2	8.15^6	7.15^9	7.1^{11}	6.8^6	5.15^{12}
6000	12.6^1	11.6^{11}	10.9^1	9.4^9	8.4^1	7.6^4	6.12^9	6.3^1
6200	12.12^{10}	11.12^{11}	10.15^8	9.9^{11}	8.8^6	7.10^{15}	6.15^9	6.6^7
6400	13.3^4	12.3^1	11.5^2	9.14^7	8.12^{14}	7.14^{15}	7.3^1	6.9^{10}
6600	13.9^{14}	12.9^1	11.10^{12}	10.3^7	9.1^5	8.2^{10}	7.7^6	6.12^{15}
6800	14.0^9	12.15^4	12.0^9	10.8^6	9.5^{10}	8.6^9	7.10^8	7.0^4
7000	14.7^2	13.5^5	12.6^3	10.13^5	9.10^1	8.10^{10}	7.13^6	7.2^{11}
7200	14.12^7	13.10^4	12.10^{10}	11.1^5	9.13^9	8.13^{13}	8.0^{15}	7.6^3
7400	......	14.1^8	11.7^1	11.7^1	10.2^{14}	9.2^9	8.5^4	7.10^5
7600	......	14.7^9	13.7^4	11.12^3	10.7^5	9.7^{12}	8.8^{14}	7.13^7
7800	......	......	13.12^{11}	12.1^2	10.11^{12}	9.10^8	8.12^7	8.0^{12}
8000	......	......	14.2^6	12.6^1	11.0^2	9.14^8	9.0^1	8.4^1
8200	......	......	......	12.11^1	11.4^9	10.2^7	9.3^{11}	8.7^6
8400	......	......	......	13.—	11.8^{14}	10.6^6	9.7^4	8.10^{10}
8600	......	......	......	......	11.13^9	10.9^{10}	9.11^1	8.13^{15}
8800	......	......	......	......	12.1^7	10.14^5	9.14^6	9.1^4
9000	......	......	......	......	......	11.2^4	10.2^1	9.4^9

Above table is figured for 2-ply yarns and includes 4 per cent. for waste.

Sizes are in English numbers and paralleled in drams; **Spun Silk** Yarns, however, have half the numbers of drams and half the weight their numbers indicate. i. e.: for a warp of 4,000 ends we have to figure the weight for a Spun Silk Warp as 2,000 ends.

FILLING WEIGHT TABLES

WIDTH: 20 In.
In Reed.

LENGTH: 100 Yds.

FILLING WEIGHT TABLE

For the Use of Tram, in a Piece of 100 Yards, 20 Inches Wide.

Picks per Inch	Deniers 22/24	24/26	28/30	30/32	32/34	36/38	40/42	42/44	44/46
	Drams 1⅜	1½	1⅝	1¾	2	2¼	2⅜	2½	2⅝
	Pounds, Ounces and Drams								
60	11	12	14	15	1.–	1.1	1.3	1.4	1.5
64	11^{12}	12^{13}	15	1.0^{1}	1.1^{7}	1.2^{8}	1.4^{5}	1.5^{6}	1.6^{8}
68	12^{9}	13^{11}	15^{15}	1.1^{2}	1.2^{4}	1.3^{6}	1.5^{11}	1.6^{8}	1.7^{15}
72	13^{4}	14^{7}	1.0^{13}	1.2^{1}	1.3^{4}	1.4^{7}	1.6^{14}	1.8^{1}	1.9^{4}
76	14	15^{4}	1.1^{13}	1.3^{2}	1.4^{6}	1.5^{10}	1.8^{3}	1.9^{7}	1.10^{2}
80	14^{11}	1.–	1.2^{11}	1.4^{1}	1.5^{8}	1.6^{11}	1.9^{6}	1.10^{11}	1.12^{4}
84	15^{7}	1.0^{4}	1.3^{11}	1.5^{1}	1.6^{8}	1.7^{11}	1.10^{1}	1.12^{2}	1.13^{8}
88	1.0^{2}	1.1^{10}	1.4^{9}	1.6	1.7^{8}	1.8^{15}	1.11^{14}	1.13^{6}	1.14^{13}
92	1.0^{15}	1.2^{7}	1.5^{9}	1.7^{1}	1.8^{10}	1.10^{3}	1.13^{4}	1.14^{13}	2.0^{5}
96	1.1^{10}	1.3^{4}	1.6^{7}	1.8	1.9^{10}	1.11^{4}	1.14^{7}	2.–	2.1^{13}
100	1.2^{6}	1.4^{4}	1.7^{6}	1.9^{1}	1.10^{12}	1.12^{8}	1.15^{12}	2.1^{7}	2.3^{2}
104	1.3^{2}	1.4^{14}	1.8^{6}	1.10^{7}	1.11^{14}	1.13^{10}	2.1^{3}	2.2^{13}	2.4^{9}
108	1.3^{14}	1.5^{10}	1.9^{4}	1.11^{1}	1.12^{14}	1.14^{11}	2.2^{4}	2.4^{2}	2.5^{14}
112	1.4^{10}	1.6^{8}	1.10^{4}	1.12^{2}	1.14	1.15^{14}	2.3^{10}	2.5^{8}	2.7^{6}
116	1.5^{5}	1.7^{4}	1.11^{2}	1.13^{1}	1.15	2.0^{15}	2.4^{13}	2.6^{12}	2.8^{11}
120	1.6	1.8	1.12	1.14	2.–	2.2	2.6	2.8	2.10
124	1.7	1.9	1.13	1.15^{1}	2.1^{2}	2.3^{2}	2.7^{5}	2.9^{6}	2.11^{6}
128	1.7^{8}	1.9^{10}	1.14	2.0^{2}	2.2^{4}	2.4^{6}	2.8^{10}	2.10^{12}	2.13
132	1.8^{4}	1.10^{8}	1.15	2.1^{5}	2.3^{6}	2.5^{9}	2.10^{4}	2.11^{14}	2.14^{7}
136	1.9^{2}	1.11^{6}	1.15^{14}	2.2^{5}	2.4^{9}	2.6^{12}	2.11^{6}	2.13	2.15^{14}
140	1.9^{12}	1.12^{2}	1.16^{12}	2.3^{3}	2.5^{9}	2.7^{13}	2.12^{9}	2.14^{12}	3.0^{11}
144	1.10^{8}	1.12^{11}	2.1^{10}	2.4^{2}	2.6^{8}	2.8^{14}	2.13^{12}	3.0^{2}	3.2^{8}
148	1.11^{4}	1.13^{10}	2.2^{10}	2.5^{3}	2.7^{10}	2.10^{6}	2.14^{14}	3.1^{8}	3.3^{6}
152	1.12	1.14^{8}	2.3^{10}	2.6^{4}	2.8^{12}	2.11^{4}	3.0^{6}	3.2^{14}	3.4^{4}
156	1.12^{14}	1.15^{4}	2.4^{8}	2.7^{3}	2.9^{12}	2.12^{5}	3.1^{9}	3.4^{2}	3.6^{3}
160	1.13^{6}	2.–	2.5^{6}	2.8^{2}	2.10^{12}	2.13^{6}	3.2^{12}	3.5^{6}	3.8^{2}
164	1.14^{3}	2.1^{2}	2.6^{6}	2.9^{2}	2.11^{14}	2.14^{8}	3.3^{9}	3.6^{8}	3.9^{14}
168	1.14^{14}	2.1^{12}	2.7^{6}	2.10^{2}	2.13	2.15^{12}	3.4^{2}	3.8^{4}	3.11
172	1.15^{9}	2.2^{7}	2.8^{4}	2.11^{1}	2.14	3.0^{13}	3.5^{14}	3.9^{8}	3.12^{5}
176	2.0^{4}	2.3^{4}	2.9^{2}	2.12	2.15	3.1^{14}	3.7^{12}	3.10^{12}	3.13^{10}
180	2.1^{5}	2.4^{2}	2.10^{2}	2.13^{1}	3.0^{2}	3.3^{2}	3.8^{14}	3.11^{7}	3.15^{2}
184	2.1^{14}	2.4^{14}	2.11^{2}	2.14^{2}	3.1^{4}	3.4^{6}	3.10^{8}	3.13^{10}	4.0^{10}
188	2.2^{10}	2.5^{9}	2.11^{12}	2.15^{1}	3.2^{4}	3.5^{7}	3.11^{11}	3.14	4.2^{2}
192	2.3^{4}	2.6^{8}	2.12^{14}	3.–	3.3^{4}	3.6^{8}	3.12^{14}	4.–	4.3^{10}
196	2.3^{14}	2.7^{5}	2.13^{13}	3.1^{1}	3.4^{4}	3.7^{10}	3.14^{4}	4.1^{7}	4.5^{2}
200	2.4^{12}	2.8^{2}	2.14^{12}	3.2^{2}	3.5^{8}	3.9	3.15^{8}	4.2^{14}	4.6^{4}

Above weights include 7 per cent. for waste.

WIDTH: 20 IN.
IN REED.
LENGTH: 100 YDS.

FILLING WEIGHT TABLE
For the Use of Tram, in a Piece of 100 Yards, 20 Inches Wide.

Picks per Inch.	DENIERS.								
	46/49	50/59	56/65	60/64	84/88	72/75	80/84	84/88	88/92
	DRAMS.								
	2¾	3	3½	3¾	4	4¼	4¾	5	5¼
	POUNDS, OUNCES AND DRAMS.								
60	1.6	1.8	1.12	1.14	2.-	2.2	2.6	2.8	2.10
64	1.7⁸	1.9¹⁰	1.14	2.0²	2.2⁴	2.4⁶	2.8¹⁰	2.10¹²	2.13
68	1.9²	1.11⁶	1.15¹⁴	2.2⁴	2.4⁸	2.6¹²	2.11⁶	2.13	2.15¹⁴
72	1.10⁸	1.12¹⁴	2.1¹⁰	2.4²	2.6⁸	2.8¹⁴	2.13¹²	3.0²	3.2⁹
76	1.12	1.14⁸	2.3¹⁰	2.6⁴	2.8¹²	2.11⁴	3.0⁶	3.2¹¹	3.4⁴
80	1.13⁶	2.-	2.5⁶	2.8²	2.10¹²	2.13⁶	3.2¹²	3.5⁶	3.8²
84	1.14¹⁴	2.1¹²	2.7⁶	2.10²	2.13	2.15¹²	3.4²	3.8⁴	3.11
88	2.0⁴	2.3⁴	2.9²	2.12	2.15	3.1¹⁴	3.7¹²	3.10¹²	3.13¹⁰
92	2.1¹⁴	2.4¹⁴	2.11²	2.14²	3.1⁴	3.4⁶	3.10⁸	3.11¹²	4.0¹⁰
96	2.3⁴	2.6⁸	2.12¹⁴	3.-	3.3⁴	3.6⁸	3.12¹⁴	4.-	4.3¹⁰
100	2.4¹²	2.8²	2.14¹²	3.2²	3.5⁸	3.9	3.15⁸	4.2¹⁴	4.6⁴
104	2.6⁴	2.9¹²	3.0¹²	3.4⁴	3.7¹²	3.11⁴	4.2⁴	4.5¹⁰	4.9²
108	2.7¹²	2.11⁴	3.2⁸	3.6²	3.9¹²	3.13⁶	4.4⁸	4.8⁴	4.11¹²
112	2.9⁴	2.13	3.4⁸	3.8⁴	3.12	3.15¹²	4.7⁴	4.11	4.14¹²
116	2.10¹⁰	2.14⁸	3.6⁴	3.10²	3.14	4.1¹⁴	4.9¹⁰	4.13⁸	5.1⁶
120	2.12	3.0	3.8	3.12	4.-	4.4	4.12	5.-	5.4
124	2.13⁸	3.1¹⁰	3.10	3.14²	4.2⁸	4.6¹⁵	4.14⁸	5.2¹²	5.7
128	2.15	3.3⁴	3.12	4.0⁸	4.4⁸	4.8¹²	5.1⁴	5.5⁸	5.10
132	3.0²	3.4¹⁴	3.13¹⁰	4.2²	4.6¹²	4.11	5.3¹⁵	5.7¹²	5.12¹⁴
136	3.2⁴	3.6¹²	3.15¹²	4.4⁸	4.9	4.13⁸	5.6¹²	5.10	5.15¹²
140	3.3¹⁴	3.8⁴	4.1²	4.6⁶	4.11	4.15⁹	5.9	5.13²	6.2⁴
144	3.5	3.9¹²	4.3⁴	4.8⁴	4.13	5.1¹⁰	5.11⁸	6.0⁴	6.5
148	3.6⁸	3.11⁶	4.5⁴	4.10⁶	4.15⁴	5.3¹⁴	5.13¹⁴	6.3⁸	6.6¹⁴
152	3.8	3.13	4.7⁴	4.12⁸	5.1⁸	5.6⁸	6.0¹²	6.5¹²	6.8⁸
156	3.9⁶	3.14⁸	4.9²	4.14⁶	5.3⁸	5.8¹⁰	6.3¹⁰	6.8⁴	6.12⁶
160	3.10¹²	4.-	4.10¹²	5.0⁴	5.5⁸	5.10¹²	6.5⁸	6.10¹²	7.0⁴
164	3.11⁸	4.1¹⁵	4.12¹²	5.2⁴	5.8⁴	5.13¹⁰	6.7¹²	6.13¹⁰	7.3²
168	3.13¹²	4.3⁸	4.14¹²	5.4⁴	5.10	5.15⁰	6.8⁴	7.0⁸	7.6
172	3.15¹⁰	4.5	5.0¹⁰	5.6²	5.12	6.1¹⁰	6.11¹⁴	7.3	7.8¹³
176	4.0⁸	4.6⁸	5.2⁴	5.8	5.14	6.3¹²	6.15⁸	7.5⁸	7.11⁴
180	4.1¹²	4.8²	5.4⁴	5.10²	6.0⁴	6.6	7.2⁸	7.6⁸	7.14⁸
184	4.3¹²	4.9¹²	5.6⁴	5.12⁴	6.2⁸	6.8¹²	7.5	7.7⁸	8.1⁴
188	4.5⁴	4.11²	5.8²	5.14²	6.4⁸	6.11	7.7⁶	7.12	8.4⁴
192	4.6⁸	4.13	5.9¹²	6.-	6.6⁸	6.13	7.9¹²	8.-	8.7⁴
196	4.8	4.14¹⁰	5.11¹⁰	6.2²	6.8⁸	6.15⁸	7.12⁴	8.3⁴	8.9¹²
200	4.9⁸	5.0⁴	5.13⁸	6.4⁴	6.11	7.2	7.15	8.5¹²	8.12⁸

Above weights include 7 **per cent.** for waste.

WIDTH: 20 IN, IN REED. **LENGTH: 100 YDS.**

FILLING WEIGHT TABLE

FOR THE USE OF TRAM, IN A PIECE OF 100 YARDS, 20 INCHES WIDE.

PICKS PER INCH.	DENIERS.								
	92/96	100/104	112/120	120/128	128/136	144/152	160/168	176/184	200/208
	DRAMS.								
	5½	6	7	7½	8	8½	9½	10½	12
	POUNDS, OUNCES AND DRAMS.								
60	2.12	3.—	3.8	3.12	4.—	4.4	4.12	5.4	6
64	2.15	3.3⁴	3.12	4.0⁴	4.4⁸	4.8¹²	5.1⁴	5.10	6.6⁸
68	3.2⁴	3.6¹²	3.15¹²	4.4⁸	4.9	4.13⁸	5.6¹²	5.15¹²	6.13⁸
72	3.5	3.9¹²	4.3⁴	4.8⁴	4.13	5.1¹⁰	5.11⁸	6.5	7.3⁸
76	3.8	3.13	4.7⁴	4.12⁸	5.1⁸	5.6⁸	6.0¹²	6.8⁸	7.10
80	3.10¹²	4.—	4.10¹²	5.0⁴	5.5⁸	5.10¹²	6.5⁸	7.0⁴	8.—
84	3.13¹²	4.3⁸	4.14¹²	5.4⁴	5.10	5.15⁸	6.8⁴	7.6	8 7
88	4.0⁸	4.6⁸	5.2⁴	5.8	5.14	6.3¹²	6.15⁸	7.11⁴	8.13
92	4.3¹²	4.9¹²	5.6⁴	5.12⁴	6.2⁸	6.8¹²	7.5	8.1⁴	9.3⁸
96	4.6⁸	4.13	5.9¹²	6.—	6.6⁸	6.13	7.9¹²	8 7⁴	9.9¹²
100	4.9⁸	5.0⁴	5.13⁸	6.4⁴	6.11	7.2	7.15	8.12⁸	10.0⁸
104	4.12⁸	5.3⁸	6.1⁸	6.8⁸	6.15⁸	7.6⁸	8.4⁸	9.2⁴	10.7
108	4.15⁸	5.6⁸	6.5	6.12⁴	7.3⁸	7.10¹²	8.9	9.7⁸	10.13
112	5.2⁸	5.10	6.9	7.0⁸	7.8	7.15⁸	8.14⁸	9.13⁸	11.4
116	5.5⁴	5.13	6.12⁸	7.4⁸	7.12	8.3¹²	9.3⁸	10.2¹²	11.10
120	5.8	6.—	7.—	7.8	8.—	8.8	9.8	10.8	12.—
124	5.11	6.3⁴	7.4	7.15¹³	8.4¹⁴	8.13	9.12¹⁴	10.14	12.7
128	5.14	6 6⁸	7.8	8.0⁸	8.9	9.1⁸	10.2⁸	11.4	12 13
132	6.1⁴	6.9¹⁵	7.11¹⁵	8.4¹⁴	8.13¹⁴	9.6⁸	10.8⁵	11.9¹²	13.5
136	6.4⁸	6.13⁸	7.15⁸	8.9	9.2	9.11	10.13⁸	11.15⁸	13.11
140	6.7⁴	7.0⁸	8.2⁴	8.13	9.6	9.15²	11.2	12.4⁸	14.1
144	6.10	7.3⁸	8.6⁸	9.0⁸	9.10	10.3⁴	11.7	12.10	14.7
148	6.13	7.7	8.10⁸	9.3⁴	9.14⁸	10.8²	11.12⁴	12.13⁷	14.13⁶
152	7.—	7.10	8.14⁸	9.6	10.3	10.13	12.1⁸	13.1	15 4
156	7.3⁴	7.13	9.2	9.11⁴	10.7	11.1⁴	12.5⁴	13.8⁴	15.10
160	7.5⁸	8.—	9.5⁸	10.0⁸	10.11	11.5⁸	12.11	14.0⁸	16.—
164	7.8⁸	8.3⁸	9.9⁸	10.4⁸	11.0⁸	11.10⁴	12.13⁸	14.6⁴	16.7
168	7.11⁸	8.7	9.13⁸	10.8⁸	11.4	11.15	13.0⁸	14.12	16.14
172	7.14⁴	8.10	10.0¹⁴	10.12⁴	11.8	12.3⁴	13.7¹⁰	15.2⁴	17.4
176	8.1	8.13	10.4⁸	11.—	11.12	12.7⁸	13.15 ·	15 6⁸	17.10
180	8.4⁴	9.0⁴	10.8⁸	11.4⁴	12.0⁸	12.1⁸	14.4⁸	15.12⁸	18.0⁸
184	8 7⁸	9.3⁸	10.12⁸	11.8⁸	12.5	13.1⁸	14.10	16.2⁸	18.7
188	8.10⁸	9.7⁴	11.—	11.12⁴	12.9	13.5¹⁴	14.14⁸	16.8⁸	18.13⁴
192	8.13⁴	9 10	11.3⁸	12.—	12.13	13.10	15.3⁸	16.14⁸	19.3⁸
196	9.—	9.13⁴	11.7⁴	12.4⁴	13.1⁸	13.15	15.8⁸	17.3¹⁰	19.10⁴
200	9.3	10 0⁸	11.11	12.8⁸	13.6	14.4	15.14	17.9	20.1

Above weights include 7 per cent. for waste.

WIDTH: 24 IN.   LENGTH: 100 YDS.
IN REED.

FILLING WEIGHT TABLE

For the Use of Tram, in a Piece of 100 Yards, 24 Inches Wide.

PICKS PER INCH.	DENIERS								
	22/24	24/26	28/30	30/32	32/34	36/38	40/42	42/44	44/46
	DRAMS								
	1$\frac{3}{8}$	1$\frac{1}{2}$	1$\frac{3}{4}$	1$\frac{7}{8}$	2	2$\frac{1}{8}$	2$\frac{3}{8}$	2$\frac{1}{2}$	2$\frac{5}{8}$
	POUNDS, OUNCES AND DRAMS.								
60	13³	14⁷	1.0¹³	1.2	1.3⁴	1.4⁷	1.6¹³	1.8¹	1.9⁴
64	14¹	15⁶	1.1¹⁵	1.3⁴	1.4⁸	1.5¹²	1.8⁵	1.9¹⁰	1.10¹⁴
68	15¹	16¹²	1.3²	1.4⁸	1.5¹⁴	1.7⁴	1.10	1.11⁶	1.12¹¹
72	15¹⁴	1.1⁶	1.4⁴	1.5¹¹	1.7²	1.8⁹	1.11⁷	1.12¹⁵	1.14⁶
76	1.0¹²	1.2⁵	1.5⁵	1.6¹⁴	1.8⁶	1.9¹⁴	1.12¹⁵	1.14⁸	2.–
80	1.1¹⁰	1.3⁵	1.6⁷	1.8	1.9¹⁰	1.11⁴	1.14⁷	2.0¹	2.1¹⁰
84	1.2⁹	1.4⁴	1.7¹⁰	1.9⁵	1.11	1.12¹¹	2.0¹	2.1¹²	2.3⁷
88	1.3⁷	1.5³	1.8¹¹	1.10⁸	1.12⁴	1.14	2.1⁹	2.3⁵	2.5¹
92	1.4⁴	1.6²	1.9¹³	1.11¹¹	1.13⁸	1.15⁵	2.3	2.4¹⁴	2.6¹¹
96	1.5³	1.7²	1.11	1.12¹⁵	1.14¹⁴	2.0⁵	2.4⁵	2.6¹⁰	2.8⁸
100	1.6¹	1.8¹	1.12²	1.14²	2.0⁵	2.2²	2.6³	2.8²	2.10²
104	1.6¹⁵	1.9	1.13³	1.15⁵	2.1⁶	2.3⁷	2.7¹¹	2.9¹²	2.11¹³
108	1.7¹³	1.9¹⁵	1.14⁵	2.0⁹	2.2¹⁰	2.4¹²	2.9²	2.11⁵	2.13⁷
112	1.8¹²	1.11	1.15⁸	2.1¹²	2.2⁴	2.6⁴	2.10¹²	2.13	2.15⁴
116	1.9¹⁰	1.11¹⁵	2.0⁹	2.2¹⁵	2.5⁴	2.7⁹	2.12⁴	2.14⁹	3.0¹⁴
120	1.10⁷	1.12¹⁴	2.1¹¹	2.4¹	2.6⁸	2.8¹⁴	2.13¹¹	3.0²	3.2⁹
124	1.11⁵	1.13¹	2.2¹³	2.5⁶	2.7¹³	2.10⁴	2.14³	3.1¹³	3.4³
128	1.12³	1.14¹²	2.3¹⁴	2.6⁷	2.9¹	2.11⁹	3.0¹⁴	3.3⁴	3.5¹³
132	1.13²	1.15¹²	2.5¹	2.7¹²	2.10⁷	2.13	3.2⁵	3.5	3.7¹⁰
136	1.14	2.0¹¹	2.6³	2.8¹⁴	2.11¹¹	2.14¹⁵	3.3¹²	3.6⁹	3.9³
140	1.15	2.1¹²	2.7⁶	2.10³	2.13	2.15¹³	3.5⁷	3.8⁴	3.11¹
144	1.15¹¹	2.2¹⁰	2.8⁶	2.11⁵	2.14⁵	3.1¹	3.6¹³	3.9¹²	3.12¹⁰
148	2.0¹¹	2.3¹⁰	2.9⁹	2.12⁹	2.15⁸	3.2⁸	3.8⁶	3.11⁶	3.14⁶
152	2.1⁸	2.4⁹	2.10¹⁰	2.13¹¹	3.0¹²	3.3¹³	3.9¹⁴	3.12¹⁵	4.–
156	2.2⁶	2.5⁸	2.11¹²	2.14¹⁴	3.2	3.5²	3.11⁶	3.14⁸	4.1¹⁰
160	2.3¹	2.6⁸	2.12¹⁴	3.0¹	3.3⁵	3.6⁸	3.12¹⁴	4.0¹	4.3⁵
164	2.4¹	2.7⁷	2.14¹⁴	3.1³	3.4¹⁰	3.7¹²	3.14⁵	4.1¹²	4.4¹⁴
168	2.5¹	2.8¹	2.15²	3.2⁸	3.5¹⁴	3.9¹	4.0¹	4.3⁵	4.6¹¹
172	2.6	2.9⁷	3.0⁵	3.3¹³	3.7⁴	3.10¹¹	4.1¹⁰	4.5¹	4.8⁸
176	2.6¹³	2.10⁶	3.1⁷	3.4¹⁵	3.8⁸	3.12	4.3¹	4.6¹⁰	4.10²
180	2.7¹⁰	2.11⁵	3.2⁸	3.6¹	3.9¹²	3.13⁵	4.4⁸	4.8⁵	4.11¹²
184	2.8⁵	2.12³	3.3¹⁰	3.7⁵	3.11²	3.14¹³	4.6³	4.9¹⁴	4.13¹⁰
188	2.9⁸	2.13⁴	3.4¹³	3.8¹⁰	3.12⁶	4.0²	4.7¹¹	4.11⁷	4.15⁴
192	2.10⁶	2.14⁸	3.5¹⁵	3.9¹²	3.13¹⁰	4.1⁷	4.9⁵	4.13	5.0¹⁴
196	2.11⁴	2.15²	3.7	3.10¹⁵	3.14¹⁴	4.2¹³	4.10¹¹	4.14¹⁰	5.2⁸
200	2.12³	3.0³	3.8³	3.12¹	4.0¹	4.4⁴	4.12⁵	5.0⁵	5.4⁵

Above weights include 7 per cent. for waste.

WIDTH: 24 IN. IN REED. **LENGTH: 100 YDS.**

FILLING WEIGHT TABLE

FOR THE USE OF TRAM, IN A PIECE OF 100 YARDS, 24 INCHES WIDE.

PICKS PER INCH	DENIERS 46/48	50/52	56/60	60/64	64/68	72/76	80/84	84/88	88/92
	DRAMS 2¾	3	3½	3¾	4	4¼	4⅝	5	5¼
	POUNDS, OUNCES AND DRAMS								
60	1.10[7]	1.12[14]	2.1[11]	2.4[1]	2.6[8]	2.8[14]	2.13[11]	3.0[2]	3.2[9]
64	1.12[3]	1.14[12]	2.3[14]	2.6[7]	2.9[1]	2.11[9]	3.0[15]	3.3[5]	3.5[13]
68	1.14[1]	2.0[13]	2.6[5]	2.9	2.11[12]	2.14[8]	3.2[15]	3.6[11]	3.9[7]
72	1.15[13]	2.2[11]	2.8[8]	2.11[6]	2.14[4]	3.1[2]	3.6[1]	3.9[13]	3.12[11]
76	2.1[8]	2.4[9]	2.10[10]	2.13[11]	3.0[12]	3.3[13]	3.9[14]	3.12[15]	4.-
80	2.3[4]	2.6[7]	2.12[14]	3.0[1]	3.3[4]	3.6[7]	3.12[14]	4.0[1]	4.3[4]
84	2.5[2]	2.8[6]	2.15[4]	3.2[5]	3.6	3.9[6]	4.0[2]	4.3[8]	4.6[14]
88	2.6[13]	2.10[6]	3.1[7]	3.4[15]	3.8[8]	3.12	4.3[1]	4.6[10]	4.10[2]
92	2.8[9]	2.12[1]	3.3[10]	3.7[5]	3.11	3.14[11]	4.6[1]	4.9[12]	4.13[7]
96	2.10[7]	2.14[5]	3.6	3.9[14]	3.13[12]	4.1[9]	4.9[5]	4.13[3]	5.1[1]
100	2.12[3]	3.0[3]	3.8[2]	3.12[4]	4.0[1]	4.4[1]	4.12[4]	5.0[5]	5.4[5]
104	2.13[14]	3.2[1]	3.10[9]	3.14[9]	4.2[12]	4.6[15]	4.15[4]	5.3[7]	5.7[10]
108	2.15[10]	3.3[15]	3.12[9]	4.0[15]	4.5[4]	4.9[9]	5.2[4]	5.6[9]	5.10[14]
112	3.1[8]	3.6	3.15	4.3[8]	4.8	4.12[8]	5.5[8]	5.10	5.14[8]
116	3.3[3]	3.7[14]	4.1[3]	4.5[13]	4.10[8]	4.15[2]	5.8[7]	5.13[2]	6.1[12]
120	3.4[13]	3.9[12]	4.3[8]	4.8[3]	4.13	5.1[13]	5.11[7]	6.0[1]	6.5[1]
124	3.6[12]	3.11[12]	4.5[11]	4.10[11]	4.15[11]	5.4[10]	5.14[10]	6.3[10]	6.8[9]
128	3.8[6]	3.13[10]	4.7[12]	4.12[14]	5.2[2]	5.7[2]	6.1[6]	6.6[11]	6.11[10]
132	3.10[1]	3.15	4.10[3]	4.15[8]	5.4[15]	5.10[1]	6.4[11]	6.10[1]	6.15[6]
136	3.12	4.1[7]	4.12[6]	5.1[11]	5.7[4]	5.12[12]	6.7[10]	6.13[2]	7.2[9]
140	3.13[14]	4.3[8]	4.14[12]	5.4[6]	5.10	5.15[10]	6.10[14]	7.0[8]	7.6[2]
144	3.15[8]	4.5[5]	5.0[15]	5.6[10]	5.12[6]	6.2[2]	6.13[11]	7.3[8]	7.9[1]
148	4.1[5]	4.7[4]	5.3[2]	5.9[1]	5.15	6.4[15]	7.0[13]	7.6[12]	7.12[11]
152	4.3	4.9[2]	5.5[5]	5.11[6]	6.1[8]	6.7[9]	7.4[11]	7.9[11]	7.15[15]
156	4.4[12]	4.11	5.7[9]	5.13[12]	6.4	6.10[1]	7.6[12]	7.13	8.3[4]
160	4.6[9]	4.12[14]	5.9[11]	6.0[4]	6.6[10]	6.13[1]	7.9[15]	8.0[6]	8.8
164	4.8[5]	4.14[15]	5.12[1]	6.2[10]	6.9[4]	6.15[12]	7.12[11]	8.3[9]	8.10[1]
168	4.10[1]	5.0[13]	5.14[4]	6.5	6.11[12]	7.2[8]	7.15[15]	8.6[11]	8.13[7]
172	4.11[13]	5.2[14]	6.0[1]	6.7[9]	6.14	7.5[6]	8.3[1]	8.10[2]	9.1
176	4.13[11]	5.4[12]	6.2[4]	6.9[15]	7.1	7.8[1]	8.6[3]	8.13[4]	9.5[5]
180	4.15[6]	5.6[10]	6.5[1]	6.12[1]	7.3[8]	7.10[12]	8.9[2]	9.0[6]	9.7[9]
184	5.1[5]	5.8[11]	6.7[7]	6.14[14]	7.6[4]	7.13[10]	8.12[7]	9.3[13]	9.11[8]
188	5.3	5.10[9]	6.9[10]	7.1[9]	7.8[12]	8.0[3]	8.15[6]	9.6[15]	9.14[8]
192	5.4[12]	5.12[7]	6.11[11]	7.3[9]	7.11[4]	8.2[15]	9.2[6]	9.10[1]	10.1[12]
196	5.6[7]	5.14[5]	6.14	7.5[14]	7.13[12]	8.5[10]	9.5[5]	9.13[3]	10.5[4]
200	5.8[5]	6.0[6]	7.0[7]	7.8[7]	8.0[5]	8.8[3]	9.8[9]	10.0[10]	10.8[10]

Above weights include 7 per cent. for waste.

WIDTH: 24 IN. IN REED. **LENGTH: 100 YDS.**

FILLING WEIGHT TABLE

For the use of Tram, in a piece of 100 yards, 24 inches wide.

Picks Per Inch.	DENIERS.							
	92/96	100/104	112/120	120/128	132/144	144/152	160/168	168/176
	DRAMS.							
	5½	6	7	7½	8	8½	9½	10
	POUNDS, OUNCES AND DRAMS.							
60	3.4^{15}	3.9^{12}	4.3^{6}	4.8^{3}	4.13	5.1^{13}	5.11^{6}	6.0^{4}
64	3.87	3.13^{9}	4.7^{14}	4.12^{15}	5.2^{2}	5.7^{3}	6.1^{6}	6.6^{10}
68	3.12^{2}	4.1^{10}	4.12^{9}	5.2^{1}	5.7^{8}	5.13	6.5^{14}	6.13^{6}
72	3.15^{10}	4.5^{8}	5.0^{15}	5.6^{12}	5.12^{8}	6.2^{5}	6.12^{8}	7.3^{10}
76	4.3	4.9^{2}	5.5^{5}	5.11^{6}	6.1^{8}	6.7^{9}	7.3^{12}	7.9^{15}
80	4.6^{7}	4.12^{14}	5.9^{11}	6.0^{7}	6.6^{8}	6.12^{14}	7.9^{12}	8.0^{2}
84	4.10^{4}	5.1	5.14^{8}	6.5^{1}	6.12	7.2^{4}	8.0^{1}	8.7
88	4.13^{11}	5.4^{12}	6.2^{14}	6.9^{15}	7.1	7.8^{1}	8.6^{2}	8.13^{4}
92	5.1^{2}	5.8^{8}	6.7^{4}	6.14^{10}	7.6	7.13^{1}	8.12^{7}	9.3^{8}
96	5.4^{14}	5.12^{10}	6.12^{1}	7.3^{12}	7.11^{8}	8.3^{5}	9.2^{10}	9.10^{6}
100	5.8^{5}	6.0^{6}	7.—	7.8^{7}	8.0^{8}	8.8^{8}	9.8^{8}	10.0^{10}
104	5.11^{13}	6.4^{2}	7.4^{13}	7.13^{7}	8.5^{8}	8.13^{15}	9.14^{9}	10.6^{14}
108	5.15^{3}	6.7^{14}	7.9^{8}	8.1^{14}	8.10^{8}	9.3^{2}	10.4^{7}	10.13^{2}
112	6.3	6.12	7.14	8.7	9.—	9.9	10.11	11.4
116	6.6^{7}	6.15^{12}	8.2^{6}	8.11^{11}	9.5	9.14^{3}	11.0^{14}	11.10^{4}
120	6.9^{14}	7.3^{8}	8.6^{12}	9.0^{6}	9.10	10.3^{10}	11.6^{14}	12.0^{8}
124	6.13^{9}	7.7^{9}	8.11^{8}	9.5^{7}	9.15^{7}	10.9^{3}	11.13^{1}	12.7^{1}
128	7.0^{12}	7.11^{4}	8.15^{12}	9.6^{6}	10.4^{5}	10.14^{4}	12.2^{12}	12.13^{4}
132	7.4^{10}	7.15^{13}	9.4^{10}	9.15^{1}	10.9^{12}	11.4^{7}	12.9^{6}	13.4^{2}
136	7.7^{6}	8.2^{15}	9.8^{12}	10.3^{11}	10.14^{9}	11.9^{6}	12.15^{6}	13.10^{1}
140	7.11^{12}	8.7	9.13^{8}	10.8^{12}	11.4	11.15^{1}	13.5^{12}	14.1
144	7.15	8.10^{6}	10.1^{13}	10.13^{4}	11.8^{13}	12.4^{14}	13.11^{6}	14.7
148	8.2^{10}	8.14^{8}	10.6^{4}	11.2^{2}	11.14	12.9^{14}	14.1^{10}	14.13^{8}
152	8.6^{1}	9.2^{4}	10.9^{4}	11.6^{13}	12.3	12.15^{3}	14.9^{6}	15.3^{10}
156	8.9^{8}	9.6	10.15	11.11^{8}	12.8	13.4^{6}	14.13^{6}	15.10
160	8.13^{3}	9.12^{8}	11.3^{13}	12.0^{9}	12.13^{6}	13.10^{3}	15.3^{14}	16.0^{12}
164	9.0^{11}	9.13^{14}	11.8^{3}	12.5^{5}	13.2^{8}	13.15^{10}	15.9^{12}	16.7^{2}
168	9.4^{2}	10.1^{10}	11.12^{9}	12.10	13.7^{8}	14.4^{15}	15.15^{14}	16.13^{8}
172	9.7^{16}	10.5^{12}	12.1^{6}	12.15^{3}	13.13	14.10^{13}	16.6^{2}	17.4^{4}
176	9.11^{6}	10.9^{8}	12.5^{12}	13.3^{14}	14.2	15.0^{2}	16.12^{6}	17.10^{9}
180	9.14^{13}	10.13^{4}	12.11^{2}	13.8^{9}	14.7	15.5^{7}	17.2^{4}	18.0^{12}
184	10.2^{9}	11.1^{6}	12.14^{15}	13.13^{11}	14.12^{8}	15.11^{4}	17.8^{14}	18.7^{10}
188	10.6^{1}	11.5^{2}	13.3^{5}	14.2^{6}	15.1^{8}	16.0^{9}	17.14^{12}	18.13^{14}
192	10.9^{7}	11.8^{14}	13.7^{11}	14.7^{1}	15.6^{9}	16.5^{14}	18.4^{12}	19.4^{2}
196	10.12^{14}	11.12^{10}	13.12^{1}	14.11^{12}	15.11^{8}	16.11^{3}	18.10^{10}	19.10^{6}
200	11.0^{11}	12.0^{12}	14.0^{14}	15.0^{15}	16.1	17.1^{1}	19.1^{2}	20.1^{4}

Above weights include 7 per cent. for waste.

FILLING WEIGHT TABLE

WIDTH: 27½ IN. IN REED.   **LENGTH: 100 YDS.**

For the Use of Tram, in a Piece of 100 Yards, 27½ Inches Wide.

Picks per Inch.	DENIERS.								
	$\frac{27}{24}$	$\frac{24}{26}$	$\frac{28}{30}$	$\frac{30}{32}$	$\frac{32}{34}$	$\frac{36}{38}$	$\frac{40}{42}$	$\frac{42}{44}$	$\frac{44}{46}$
	DRAMS.								
	$1\frac{3}{8}$	$1\frac{1}{2}$	$1\frac{5}{8}$	$1\frac{7}{8}$	2	$2\frac{1}{8}$	$2\frac{3}{8}$	$2\frac{1}{2}$	$2\frac{5}{8}$
	POUNDS, OUNCES AND DRAMS.								
60	15^2	1.0^8	1.3^4	1.4^{10}	1.6	1.7^6	1.10^2	1.11^8	1.12^{14}
64	1.0^3	1.1^{10}	1.4^9	1.6	1.7^8	1.9	1.11^{14}	1.13^6	1.14^{13}
68	1.1^3	1.2^{12}	1.5^{14}	1.7^7	1.9	1.10^9	1.13^{11}	1.15^4	2.0^{13}
72	1.2^3	1.3^{14}	1.7^3	1.8^{13}	1.10^8	1.12^2	1.15^7	2.1^2	2.2^{12}
76	1.3^2	1.4^{14}	1.8^6	1.10^2	1.11^{14}	1.13^{10}	2.1^2	2.2^{14}	2.4^9
80	1.4^3	1.6	1.9^{11}	1.11^9	1.13^6	1.15^3	2.2^{14}	2.4^{11}	2.6^9
84	1.5^4	1.7^2	1.11	1.12^{15}	1.14^{14}	2.0^{15}	2.4^{11}	2.6^9	2.8^8
88	1.6^4	1.8^4	1.12^5	1.13^{14}	2.0^6	2.2^6	2.5^{10}	2.8^7	2.10^8
92	1.7^3	1.9^5	1.13^8	1.15^{10}	2.1^{12}	2.3^{11}	2.8^1	2.10^3	2.12^5
96	1.8^4	1.10^7	1.14^{13}	2.1^1	2.3^4	2.5^7	2.9^{14}	2.12^1	2.14^4
100	1.9^4	1.11^9	2.0^2	2.2^8	2.4^{12}	2.7^1	2.11^{10}	2.14	3.0^4
104	1.10^5	1.12^{11}	2.1^7	2.3^{14}	2.6^4	2.8^{10}	2.13^7	2.15^{13}	3.2^3
108	1.11^5	1.13^{12}	2.2^{12}	2.5^4	2.7^{12}	2.10^4	2.15^3	3.1^{11}	3.4^3
112	1.12^4	1.14^{13}	2.4	2.6^9	2.9^2	2.11^{11}	3.0^{13}	3.3^6	3.6
116	1.13^5	2.-	2.5^5	2.7^{15}	2.10^{10}	2.13^5	3.2^{10}	3.5^4	3.7^{15}
120	1.14^4	2.1	2.6^8	2.9^4	2.12	2.14^{12}	3.4^4	3.7	3.9^{12}
124	1.15^5	2.2^2	2.8^3	2.10^{12}	2.13^8	3.0^6	3.5^2	3.8^{14}	3.11^{12}
128	2.0^6	2.3^4	2.9^2	2.12	2.15	3.2	3.7^{12}	3.10^{12}	3.13^{13}
132	2.1^6	2.4^6	2.10^7	2.13^7	3.0^8	3.4	3.9^9	3.12^{10}	3.15^{11}
136	2.2^6	2.5^8	2.11^{17}	2.14^{14}	3.2	3.5^2	3.11^6	3.14^6	4.1^{10}
140	2.3^6	2.6^{10}	2.13^1	3.0^8	3.3^8	3.7	3.13^2	4.0^6	4.3^9
144	2.4^6	2.7^{12}	2.14^6	3.1^{10}	3.5	3.8^4	3.14^{14}	4.2^4	4.5^9
148	2.5^5	2.8^{12}	2.15^9	3.3^2	3.6^6	3.10^2	4.0^{10}	4.4	4.7^9
152	2.6^4	2.9^{12}	3.0^{12}	3.4^4	3.7^{12}	3.11^4	4.2^4	4.5^{13}	4.9^2
156	2.7^5	2.10^{14}	3.2^4	3.6	3.9	3.12^{13}	4.4^2	4.7^9	4.11^8
160	2.8^6	2.12	3.3^6	3.7^2	3.10^{12}	3.14^6	4.5^{12}	4.9^6	4.14^2
164	2.9^7	2.13^2	3.5^6	3.8^{10}	3.12	4.0^2	4.7^9	4.11^4	4.15^9
168	2.10^8	2.14^4	3.6	3.9^{14}	3.13^{12}	4.1^{10}	4.9^6	4.13^2	5.1
172	2.11^8	2.15^6	3.7^5	3.10^{13}	3.15	4.3	4.10^5	4.15^2	5.3
176	2.12^8	3.0^8	3.8^{10}	3.11^{12}	4.0^{12}	4.4^{12}	4.11^4	5.0^{14}	5.5
180	2.13^7	3.1^9	3.10^1	3.13	4.2^2	4.6^2	4.13^8	5.2^8	5.7^2
184	2.14^6	3.2^{10}	3.11	3.15^4	4.3^8	4.7^9	5.0^2	5.4^6	5.8^{10}
188	2.15^7	3.3^{12}	3.12^5	4.0^{10}	4.5	4.9^6	5.2^1	5.6^5	5.9^{14}
192	3.0^8	3.4^{14}	3.13^{10}	4.2^2	4.6^6	4.10^{14}	5.3^{12}	5.8^2	5.12^8
196	3.1^8	3.6	3.14^{14}	4.3^{10}	4.8	4.12^{12}	5.5^8	5.10^1	5.14^8
200	3.2^8	3.7^2	4.0^4	4.5	4.9^8	4.14^2	5.7^4	5.12	6.0^9

Above weights include 7 per cent. for waste.

WIDTH: 27½ IN. LENGTH: 100 YDS.
IN REED.

FILLING WEIGHT TABLE

For the Use of Tram, in a Piece of 100 Yards, 27½ Inches Wide.

PICKS PER INCH	DENIERS								
	46/48	50/52	56/60	60/64	64/68	72/76	80/84	84/88	88/92
	DRAMS								
	2¼	3	3½	3¾	4	4¼	4¾	5	5¼
	POUNDS, OUNCES AND DRAMS								
60	1.14^4	2.1	2.6^8	2.9^4	2.12	2.14^{12}	3.4^4	3.7	3.9^{12}
64	2.0^6	2.3^4	2.9^2	2.12	2.15	3.2	3.7^{12}	3.10^{12}	3.13^{12}
68	2.2^6	2.5^8	2.11^{12}	2.14^{14}	3.2	3.5^2	3.11^6	3.14^9	4.1^{10}
72	2.4^6	2.7^{12}	2.14^6	3.1^{10}	3.5	3.8^4	3.14^{14}	4.2^1	4.5^9
76	2.6^4	2.9^{12}	3.0^{12}	3.4^4	3.7^{12}	3.11^4	4.2^4	4.5^{12}	4.9^2
80	2.8^6	2.12	3.3^6	3.7^2	3.10^{12}	3.14^6	4.5^{12}	4.9^6	4.14^2
84	2.10^8	2.14^4	3.6	3.9^{14}	3.13^{12}	4.1^{10}	4.9^6	4.13^2	5.1
88	2.12^8	3.0^8	3.8^{10}	3.11^{12}	4.0^{12}	4.4^{12}	4.11^4	5.0^{14}	5.5
92	2.14^6	3.2^{10}	3.11	3.15^4	4.3^8	4.7^6	5.0^2	5.4^6	5.8^{10}
96	3.0^8	3.4^{14}	3.13^{10}	4.2^2	4.6^8	4.10^{14}	5.3^{12}	5.8^2	5.12^8
100	3.2^8	3.7^2	4.0^4	4.5	4.9^8	4.14^2	5.7^4	5.12	6.0^8
104	3.4^{10}	3.9^6	4.2^{14}	4.7^{12}	4.12^8	5.1^4	5.10^{14}	5.15^{10}	6.4^6
108	3.6^{10}	3.11^{10}	4.5^8	4.10^8	4.15^8	5.4^6	5.14^6	6.3^6	6.8^8
112	3.8^6	3.13^{10}	4.8	4.13^2	5.2^4	5.7^6	6.1^{10}	6.6^{12}	6.12
116	3.10^{10}	4.—	4.10^{10}	4.15^{14}	5.5^4	5.10^{10}	6.5^4	6.10^8	6.15^{14}
120	3.12^6	4.2	4.13	5.2^8	5.8	5.13^8	6.8^9	6.14	7.3^8
124	3.14^{10}	4.4^4	5.0^6	5.5^4	5.11	6.0^4	6.11^8	6.17^8	7.7^6
128	4.0^{12}	4.6^8	5.2^4	5.8	5.14	6.4	6.15^8	7.5^9	7.11^8
132	4.2^{12}	4.8^8	5.5^2	5.11	6.0^8	6.7^2	7.3^2	7.9^4	7.15^6
136	4.4^{12}	4.11	5.7^{12}	5.13^{12}	6.4	6.10^4	7.6^{12}	7.13	8.3^4
140	4.6^{12}	4.13^4	5.10	6.0^8	6.7	6.13^4	7.10	8.1^4	8.7^2
144	4.8^{12}	4.15^8	5.12^{12}	6.3^4	6.10	7.0^8	7.13^{12}	8.4^8	8.11
148	4.10^{10}	5.0^{14}	5.15	6.5^{13}	6.13	7.3^8	8.0^{10}	8.8	8.14^2
152	4.12^8	5.3^8	6.1^8	6.8^8	6.15^8	7.6^8	8.4^9	8.11^8	9.2^4
156	4.14^{10}	5.6^4	6.4^8	6.11^6	7.2^8	7.9^{10}	8.8	8.15	9.7^4
160	5.0^{12}	5.8	6.6^{12}	6.14^4	7.5^8	7.12^{12}	8.11^8	9.2^{12}	9.12^4
164	5.3^6	5.10^4	6.9^6	7.0^{14}	7.8^8	8.0^4	8.14^{10}	9.6^8	9.15^2
168	5.6	5.12^6	6.12	7.3^{12}	7.11^8	8.3^4	9.2^{12}	9.10^4	10.2
172	5.7^8	5.15	6.14^2	7.5^{10}	7.14^8	8.6^6	9.4^{10}	9.14^1	10.6
176	5.9	6.1	7.1^4	7.7^8	8.1^8	8.9^8	9.6^6	10.1^{12}	10.10
180	5.11^1	6.3^2	7.4	7.11	8.4^7	8.12	9.5^9	10.5^8	10.13^{14}
184	5.12^{12}	6.5^4	7.6	7.14^8	8.7	8.14^{12}	10.0^4	10.8^{12}	11.1^4
188	5.14	6.7^8	7.8^7	8.1^6	8.10	9.1^{12}	10.4^2	10.12^8	11.5^2
192	6.1	6.9^{12}	7.11^4	8.4^4	8.13	9.5^{12}	10.7^8	11.0^4	11.9
196	6.3	6.11^2	7.13^4	8.7^2	9.—	9.9^2	10.10^{14}	11.4^2	11.14
200	6.5	6.14^4	8.0^8	8.10	9.3	9.12^4	10.14^8	11.8	12.1

Above weights include 7 per cent. for waste.

WIDTH: 24 IN.
IN REED.

LENGTH: 100 YDS.

FILLING WEIGHT TABLE

FOR COTTON OR SPUN SILK YARNS.

PICKS PER INCH.	DRAMS.															
	15	9¾	7½	6	5	4¼	3¾	3⅜	3	2¾	2½	2⅜	2⅛	1⅞	1¾	1½
	SIZES OF YARNS IN ENGL. No.—1-PLY.															
	20	30	40	50	60	70	80	90	100	110	120	130	140	160	180	200
	POUNDS AND OUNCES.															
60	8.15	5.15	4.7	3.9	2.15	2.9	2.3	2.–	1.13	1.10	1.8	1.6	1.4	1 2	1.–	–.14
64	9.8	6.5	4.12	3.14	3 3	2.11	2.6	2 2	1.15	1.12	1.9	1.7	1.6	1.3	1.1	–.15
68	10.2	6.12	5.1	4.–	3.6	2.12	2 9	2.4	2 –	1.13	1 11	1.9	1.7	1.4	1.2	1.–
72	10.11	7.2	5.6	4.4	3.9	3.1	2 11	2 6	2 2	1 15	1.13	1.10	1.8	1.5	1.3	1.1
76	11.5	7.8	5.10	4.8	3.12	3.4	2.13	2.8	2 4	2.1	1.14	1.12	1.10	1 7	1.4	1.2
80	11.14	7.15	5.15	4.12	3 15	3.6	2 15	2.10	2 6	2 3	2.–	1 13	1.11	1.8	1.5	1.3
84	12.8	8.5	6.4	4.15	4 3	3.9	3 2	2.12	2.8	2.4	2.1	1 15	1.13	1.9	1.6	1.4
88	13.1	8.11	6.9	5.4	4.6	3.12	3.4	2 14	2 10	2.6	2 3	2.–	1 14	1 10	1.7	1.5
92	13.11	9.2	6.13	5.7	4.9	3 14	3 7	3.1	2 12	2.8	2.4	2.2	1.15	1 11	1.8	1 6
96	14.4	9.8	7.2	5.11	4 12	4.1	3.9	3.3	2.14	2.10	2.6	2.3	2 1	1.13	1.9	1.7
100	14.15	9.14	7.7	5.15	4.15	4.4	3.11	3.5	3.–	2.11	2.8	2.5	2.2	1 14	1.10	1.8
104	15.7	10.5	7.12	6 3	5.2	4.8	3.13	3.7	3.1	2.13	2.9	2 6	2 3	1 15	1.11	1.9
108	16 –	10.11	8.–	6 7	5.5	4.9	4.–	3 9	3.3	2.15	2.11	2.7	2.5	2.–	1.13	1.10
112	16.10	11.1	8.5	6.10	5.9	4.12	4.3	3.11	3.5	3.–	2.12	2.9	2.6	2 1	1.14	1 11
116	17.4	11.8	8.10	6.14	5.12	4 15	4.5	3.13	3.7	3 2	2.14	2.10	2.7	2.2	1.15	1 12
120	17.13	11.14	8.14	7.2	5.15	5.2	4.7	3.15	3.9	3.4	3 –	2.12	2.9	2.4	2.–	1.13
124	18.7	12.5	9.3	7.6	6.2	5 4	4.10	4.1	3.11	3.6	3 1	2.13	2.10	2.5	2.1	1.14
128	19.–	12.11	9.8	7.10	6.5	5.7	4 12	4.4	3 13	3.7	3.3	2.15	2.11	2.6	2.2	1.15
132	19.10	13.1	9.13	7.14	6.9	5.9	4.14	4.6	3.15	3.9	3.4	3.–	2.13	2.7	2.3	1 15
136	20.3	13.7	10.2	8.1	6.12	5.12	5.1	4.8	4 1	3.11	3.6	3.2	2.14	2 8	2.4	2.–
140	20.13	13.14	10.6	8 5	6.15	5.15	5.3	4 10	4.3	3.13	3.7	3.3	3.–	2.10	2.5	2.1
144	21.6	14.4	10.11	8.9	7.2	6.2	5.6	4.12	4.4	3.14	3.9	3.5	3.1	2.11	2.6	2.2
148	22.–	14.11	11.–	8 13	7.5	6.5	5.8	4.14	4.6	4.–	3.11	3.6	3.2	2 12	2.7	2.3
152	22.9	15.1	11.5	9.1	7.8	6.7	5.10	5.–	4.8	4 2	3.12	3.8	3.4	2.13	2 8	2.4
156	23.3	15.7	11.9	9.4	7.12	6.10	5.13	5.2	4.10	4.3	3.14	3.9	3.5	2.14	2.9	2.5
160	23.12	15.13	11.14	9.8	7.15	6.13	5.15	5.5	4.12	4.5	3.15	3.11	3.6	3.–	2.10	2.6
164	24.6	16.4	12.3	9.12	8.2	6.15	6.1	5.7	4.14	4.7	4.1	3.12	3.8	3.1	2.11	2.7
168	24.15	16.10	12.8	9.15	8.5	7.2	6.4	5.9	5.–	4.9	4.3	3.13	3.9	3.2	2.12	2.8
172	25.9	17.1	12 12	10.4	8.8	7.5	6.6	5.11	5.2	4.10	4.4	3.15	3.10	3.3	2.13	2.9
176	26.2	17.7	13.1	10.7	8.11	7.8	6.9	5.13	5.4	4.12	4.6	4.–	3.12	3.4	2.14	2.10
180	26.12	17.13	13.6	10.11	8.15	7.10	6.11	5.15	5.6	4.14	4.7	4.2	3.13	3.5	3.–	2.11
184	27.5	18.4	13.11	10.15	9.2	7.13	6 13	6.1	5.7	5.–	4.9	4.3	3.14	3.7	3.1	2.12
188	28.–	18.10	13.15	11.3	9.5	8.–	7.–	6.3	5.9	5.1	4.10	4 5	4.–	3.8	3.2	2.13
192	28.8	19.–	14 4	11.7	9.8	8.2	7.2	6.5	5.11	5.3	4.12	4.6	4 1	3.9	3.3	2.14
196	29.2	19.7	14.9	11.10	9.11	8.5	7.4	6.8	5.13	5.5	4.14	4.8	4.3	3.10	3.4	2.15
200	29.11	19.13	14.14	11.14	9.14	8.7	7.6	6.10	5.15	5.6	4.15	4.9	4.4	3.11	3.5	3 –

Above **weights include 4 per cent. for waste.**

Above weights are for 1-ply yarns; 2-ply and 3-ply cotton yarns are respectively double and thrice the above weights and drams; **Spun Silk Yarns, however,** in 2 and 3 ply have the number of drams and the same weight their numbers indicate, and are written $^{20}/_{2}$, $^{30}/_{2}$, $^{20}/_{3}$, $^{30}/_{3}$,

REMARKS ABOUT WASTE.

The figuring of the waste in these weight tables is kept uniform.

The warp weight tables include 4 per cent., and the filling weight tables include 7 per cent., which figures are pretty exact in the manufacture of a good many articles, when best raw material is used.

Now, there are a number of goods which cause less waste during the manufacturing process, and then again many which cause more, for instance, on one side there are piece dyed goods and on the other side complicated goods with a large variety of colors, or heavy weighted and doubled fillings.

According to the quality of the raw material, and according to the nature and quality of the article to be manufactured, we sometimes have to modify the results of the weights in our calculations a few per cent., but in a great many goods the weights are correct.

Comparative Yarn Tables.

Comparative

Cotton Scale.	Yards per lb.	Yards per oz.	Yards per dram.	Metres per Kilogramme	Italian Scale in Deniers.	Manchester Scale. Drams per 1000 Yards.
1	840	52½	3·281	1,692	5,282·333	304·761
1½	1,260	78¾	4·921	2,539	3,521·555	203·174
2	1,680	105	6·562	3,384	2,641·166	152·380
2½	2,100	131¼	8·203	4,232	2,112·933	121·904
3	2,520	157½	9·843	5,078	1,760·777	101·587
3½	2,940	183¾	11·484	5,925	1,509·238	87·074
4	3,360	210	13·125	6,768	1,320·583	76·190
4½	3,780	236¼	14·765	7,617	1,173·581	67·195
5	4,200	262½	16·406	8,464	1,056·466	60·952
5½	4,620	288¾	18·046	9,310	960·422	55·411
6	5,040	315	19·687	10,157	880·388	50·793
6½	5,460	341¼	21·328	11,003	812·666	46·886
7	5,880	367½	22·968	11,850	754·619	43·537
7½	6,300	393¾	24·609	12,696	704·311	40·634
8	6,720	420	26·250	13,536	660·292	38·095
8½	7,140	446¼	27·890	14,389	621·450	35·854
9	7,560	472½	29·531	15,235	586·925	33·597
9½	7,980	498¾	31·171	16,082	556·035	32·080
10	8,400	525	32·812	16,928	528·233	30·476
10½	8,820	551¼	34·453	17,775	503·079	29·024
11	9,240	577½	36·093	18,621	480·212	27·705
11½	9,660	603¾	37·734	19,468	459·333	26·501
12	10,080	630	39·375	20,314	440·194	25·396
12½	10,500	656¼	41·015	21,161	422·586	24·380
13	10,920	682½	42·656	22,007	406·333	23·443
13½	11,340	708¾	44·296	22,853	391·283	22·574
14	11,760	735	45·937	23,700	377·309	21·768
14½	12,180	761¼	47·578	24,546	364·298	21·018
15	12,600	787½	49·218	25,393	352·156	20·317
15½	13,020	813¾	50·859	26,239	340·795	19·662
16	13,440	840	52·500	27,072	330·146	19·047
16½	13,860	866¼	54·140	27,932	320·141	18·470
17	14,280	892½	55·781	28,779	310·725	17·927
17½	14,700	918¾	57·421	29,625	301·847	17·414
18	15,120	945	59·062	30,471	293·462	16·793
18½	15,540	971¼	60·703	31,318	285·531	16·473
19	15,960	997½	62·343	32,164	278·018	16·040
19½	16,380	1,023¾	63·984	33,011	270·888	15·628
20	16,800	1,050	65·625	33,857	264·116	15·238
20½	17,220	1,076¼	67·265	34,704	257·674	14·866
21	17,640	1,102½	68·906	35,550	251·539	14·512
21½	18,060	1,128¾	70·546	36,397	245·689	14·174
22	18,480	1,155	72·187	37,243	240·106	13·852
22½	18,900	1,181¼	73·828	38,089	234·770	13·544
23	19,320	1,207½	75·468	38,936	229·666	13·250
23½	19,740	1,233¾	77·109	39,782	224·780	12·968
24	20,160	1,260	78·750	40,629	220·097	12·698
24½	20,580	1,286¼	80·390	41,475	215·604	12·439
25	21,000	1,312½	82·031	42,322	211·293	12·190

Yarn Tables.

Cotton Scale.	Linen Scale. Leas of 300 yds. in 1 lb.	Worsted Scale.	Hawick Scale Cuts of 300 yds. in 26 oz.	Galashiels Scale Cuts of 300 yds. in 24 oz.	Alloa Scale Spindles in 24 lbs.	Aberdeen Scale. lbs. per Spindle.
1	2·800	1½	4·550	4·200	1·750	17·142
1½	4·200	2¼	6·825	6·300	2·625	11·428
2	5·600	3	9·100	8·400	3·500	8·571
2½	7·000	3¾	11·375	10·500	4·375	6·857
3	8·400	4½	13·650	12·600	5·250	5·714
3½	9·800	5¼	15·925	14·700	6·125	4·897
4	11·200	6	18·200	16·800	7·000	4·285
4½	12·600	6¾	20·475	18·900	7·875	3·809
5	14·000	7½	22·750	21·000	8·750	3·428
5½	15·400	8¼	25·025	23·100	9·625	3·116
6	16·800	9	27·300	25·200	10·500	2·857
6½	18·200	9¾	29·575	27·300	11·375	2·637
7	19·600	10½	31·850	29·400	12·250	2·448
7½	21·000	11¼	34·125	31·500	13·125	2·285
8	22·400	12	36·400	33·600	14·000	2·142
8½	23·800	12¾	38·675	35·700	14·875	2·016
9	25·200	13½	40·950	37·800	15·750	1·904
9½	26·600	14¼	43·225	39·900	16·625	1·804
10	28·000	15	45·500	42·000	17·500	1·714
10½	29·400	15¾	47·775	44·100	18·375	1·632
11	30·800	16½	50·050	46·200	19·250	1·558
11½	32·200	17¼	52·325	48·300	20·125	1·490
12	33·600	18	54·600	50·400	21·000	1·428
12½	35·000	18¾	56·875	52·500	21·875	1·371
13	36·400	19½	59·150	54·600	22·750	1·318
13½	37·800	20¼	61·425	56·700	23·625	1·269
14	39·200	21	63·700	58·800	24·500	1·224
14½	40·600	21¾	65·975	60·900	25·375	1·182
15	42·000	22½	68·250	63·000	26·250	1·142
15½	43·400	23¼	70·525	65·100	27·125	1·106
16	44·800	24	72·800	67·200	28·000	1·071
16½	46·200	24¾	75·075	69·300	28·875	1·038
17	47·600	25½	77·350	71·400	29·750	1·008
17½	49·000	26¼	79·625	73·500	30·625	0·979
18	50·400	27	81·900	75·600	31·500	0·952
18½	51·800	27¾	84·175	77·700	32·375	0·926
19	53·200	28½	86·450	79·800	33·250	0·902
19½	54·600	29¼	88·725	81·900	34·125	0·879
20	56·000	30	91·000	84·000	35·000	0·857
20½	57·400	30¾	93·275	86·100	35·875	0·836
21	58·800	31½	95·550	88·200	36·750	0·816
21½	60·200	32¼	97·825	90·300	37·625	0·797
22	61·600	33	100·100	92·400	38·500	0·779
22½	63·000	33¾	102·375	94·500	39·375	0·761
23	64·400	34½	104·650	96·600	40·250	0·745
23½	65·800	35¼	106·925	98·700	41·125	0·729
24	67·200	36	109·200	100·800	42·000	0·714
24½	68·600	36¾	111·475	102·900	42·875	0·699
25	70·000	37½	113·750	105·000	43·750	0·685

Comparative Yarn Tables.

Cotton Scale.	Yards per lb.	Yards per oz.	Metres per Kilo-gramme.	Italian Scale in Deniers.	Manchester Scale. Drams per 1000 Yards.	Linen Scale Leas of 300 yds. in 1 lb.	Worsted Scale.
25½	21,420	1,338¾	43,168	207·150	11·951	71.400	38¼
26	21,840	1,365	44,015	203·166	11·721	72·800	39
26½	22,260	1,391¼	44,861	199·333	11·500	74·200	39¾
27	22,680	1,417½	45,707	195·642	11·287	75·600	40½
27½	23,100	1,443¾	46,554	192·084	11·082	77·000	41¼
28	23,520	1,470	47,400	188·654	10·884	78·400	42
28½	23,940	1,496¼	48,247	185·345	10·693	79·800	42¾
29	24,360	1,522½	49,093	182·149	10·509	81·200	43½
29½	24,780	1,548¾	49,940	179·062	10·330	82·600	44¼
30	25,200	1,575	50,786	176·078	10·158	84·000	45
30½	25,620	1,601¼	51,632	173·191	9·992	85·400	45¾
31	26,040	1,627½	52,479	170·398	9·831	86·800	46½
31½	26,460	1,653¾	53,325	167·693	9·674	88·200	47¼
32	26,880	1,680	54,144	165·073	9·523	89·600	48
32½	27,300	1,706¼	55,018	162·533	9·377	91·000	48¾
33	27,720	1,732½	55,865	160·070	9·235	92·400	49½
33½	28,140	1,758¾	56,711	157·681	9·097	93·800	50¼
34	28,560	1,785	57,558	155·362	8·963	95·200	51
34½	28,980	1,811¼	58,404	153·111	8·833	96·600	51¾
35	29,400	1,837½	59,250	150·923	8·707	98·000	52½
35½	29,820	1,863¾	60,097	148·798	8·584	99·400	53¼
36	30,240	1,890	60,943	146·731	8·399	100·800	54
36½	30,660	1,916¼	61,790	144·721	8·349	102·200	54¾
37	31,080	1,942½	62,636	142·766	8·236	103·600	55½
37½	31,500	1,968¾	63,483	140·852	8·126	105·000	56¼
38	31,920	1,995	64,329	139·009	8·020	106·400	57
38½	32,340	2,021¼	65,176	137·203	7·915	107·800	57¾
39	32,760	2,047½	66,022	135·444	7·814	109·200	58½
39½	33,180	2,073¾	66,868	133·729	7·715	110·600	59¼
40	33,600	2,100	67,715	132·058	7·619	112·000	60
40½	34,020	2,126¼	68,561	130·427	7·524	113·400	60¾
41	34,440	2,152½	69,408	128·837	7·433	114·800	61½
41½	34,860	2,178¾	70,254	127·285	7·343	116·200	62¼
42	35,280	2,205	71,101	125·769	7·256	117·600	63
42½	35,700	2,231¼	71,947	124·290	7·170	119·000	63¾
43	36,120	2,257½	72,794	122·844	7·087	120·400	64½
43½	36,540	2,283¾	73,640	121·432	7·006	121·800	65¼
44	36,960	2,310	74,486	120·053	6·926	123·200	66
44½	37,380	2,336¼	75,333	118·704	6·848	124·600	66¾
45	37,800	2,362½	76,179	117·385	6·772	126·000	67½
45½	38,220	2,388¾	77,026	116·095	6·698	127·400	68¼
46	38,640	2,415	77,872	114·833	6·625	128·800	69
46½	39,060	2,441¼	78,719	113·598	6·554	130·200	69¾
47	39,480	2,467½	79,565	112·390	6·484	131·600	70½
47½	39,900	2,493¾	80,412	111·207	6·416	133·000	71¼
48	40,320	2,520	81,258	110·048	6·349	134·400	72
48½	40,740	2,546¼	82,104	108·914	6·283	135·800	72¾
49	41,160	2,572½	82,951	107·802	6·219	137·200	73½
49½	41,580	2,598¾	83,797	106·713	6·156	138·600	74¼
50	42,000	2,625	84,644	105·566	6·095	140·000	75

Comparative Yarn Tables.

Cotton Scale.	Yards per lb.	Yards per oz.	Metres per Kilogramme.	Italian Scale in Deniers.	Manchester Scale. Drams per 1000 yds.	Linen Scale Leas of 300 yds. in 1 lb.	Worsted Scale.
51	42,840	2,677½	86,337	103·575	5·975	142·800	76½
52	43,680	2,730	88,030	101·583	5·860	145·600	78
53	44,520	2,782½	89,722	99·666	5·750	148·400	79½
54	45,360	2,835	91,415	97·821	5·643	151·200	81
55	46,200	2,887½	93,108	96·042	5·541	154·000	82½
56	47,040	2,940	94,801	94·327	5·442	156·800	84
57	47,880	2,992½	96,494	92·672	5·346	159·600	85½
58	48,720	3,045	98,195	91·075	5·254	162·400	87
59	49,560	3,097½	99,880	89·531	5·165	165·200	88½
60	50,400	3,150	101,573	88·039	5·079	168·000	90
61	51,240	3,202½	103,265	86·595	4·996	170·800	91½
62	52,080	3,255	104,958	85·199	4·915	173·600	93
63	52,920	3,307½	106,651	83·846	4·837	176·400	94½
64	53,760	3,360	108,288	82·536	4·761	179·200	96
65	54,600	3,412½	110,037	81·266	4·688	182·000	97½
66	55,440	3,465	111,730	80·035	4·617	184·800	99
67	56,280	3,517½	113,423	78·840	4·548	187·600	100½
68	57,120	3,570	115,116	77·681	4·481	190·400	102
69	57,960	3,622½	116,809	76·555	4·416	193·200	103½
70	58,800	3,675	118,501	75·462	4·353	196·000	105
71	59,640	3,727½	120,194	74·399	4·292	198·800	106½
72	60,480	3,780	121,887	73·366	4·299	201·600	108
73	61,320	3,832½	123,580	72·360	4·174	204·400	109½
74	62,160	3,885	125,272	71·383	4·118	207·200	111
75	63,000	3,937½	126,966	70·431	4·063	210·000	112½
76	63,840	3,990	128,659	69·504	4·010	212·800	114
77	64,680	4,042½	130,352	68·601	3·957	215·600	115½
78	65,520	4,095	132,045	67·722	3·907	218·400	117
79	66,360	4,147½	133,737	66·864	3·857	221·200	118½
80	67,200	4,200	135,430	66·029	3·809	224·000	120
81	68,040	4,252½	137,123	65·213	3·762	226·800	121½
82	68,880	4,305	138,816	64·418	3·716	229·600	123
83	69,720	4,357½	140,509	63·642	3·671	232·400	124½
84	70,560	4,410	142,202	62·884	3·628	235·200	126
85	71,400	4,462½	143,895	62·145	3·585	238·000	127½
86	72,240	4,515	145,588	61·422	3·543	240·800	129
87	73,080	4,567½	147,280	60·716	3·503	243·600	130½
88	73,920	4,620	148,973	60·026	3·463	246·400	132
89	74,760	4,672½	150,666	59·352	3·424	249·200	133½
90	75,600	4,725	152,359	58·692	3·386	252·000	135
91	76,440	4,777½	154,052	58·047	3·349	254·800	136½
92	77,280	4,830	155,744	57·416	3·312	257·600	138
93	78,120	4,882½	157,438	56·799	3·277	260·400	139½
94	78,960	4,935	159,131	56·195	3·242	263·200	141
95	79,800	4,987½	160,824	55·603	3·208	266·000	142½
96	80,640	5,040	162,516	55·024	3·174	268·800	144
97	81,480	5,092½	164,209	54·457	3·141	271·600	145½
98	82,320	5,145	165,902	53·901	3·109	274·400	147
99	83,160	5,197½	167,595	53·356	3·078	277·200	148½
100	84,000	5,250	169,288	52·783	3·047	280·000	150

Comparative Yarn Tables.

Cotton Scale.	Yards per lb.	Yards per oz.	Metres per Kilo- gramme.	Italian Scale in Deniers.	Manchester Scale. Drams per 1000 yds.	Linen Scale. Leas of 300 yds. in 1 lb.
105	88,200	5,512½	177,752	50·307	2·992	294·000
110	92,400	5,775	186,217	48·021	2·770	308·000
115	96,600	6,037½	194,681	45·933	2·650	322·000
120	100,800	6,300	203,146	44·019	2·539	336·000
125	105,000	6,562½	211,610	42·258	2·438	350·000
130	109,200	6,825	220,075	40·633	2·344	364·000
135	113,400	7,087½	228,539	39·128	2·257	378·000
140	117,600	7,350	237,003	37·731	2,176	392·000
145	121,800	7,612½	245,468	36·429	2·101	406·000
150	126,000	7,875	253,932	35·215	2·031	420·000
155	130,200	8,137½	262,397	34·079	1·966	434·000
160	134,400	8,400	270,861	33·014	1·904	448·000
165	138,600	8,662½	279,326	32·014	1·847	462·000
170	142,800	8,925	287,790	31·072	1·792	476·000
175	147,000	9,187½	296,254	30·184	1·741	490·000
180	151,200	9,450	304,719	29·346	1·693	504·000
185	155,400	9,712½	313,183	28·553	1·647	518·000
190	159,600	9,975	321,648	27·801	1·604	532·000
195	163,800	10,237½	330,112	27·088	1·562	546·000
200	168,000	10,500	338,577	26·392	1·523	560·000
205	172,200	10,762½	347,041	25·767	1·486	574·000
210	176,400	11,025	355,505	25·154	1·451	588·000
215	180,600	11,287½	363,970	24·568	1·417	602·000
220	184,800	11,550	372,432	24·010	1·385	616·000
225	189,000	11,812½	380,898	23·477	1·354	630·000
230	193,200	12,075	389,363	22·966	1·325	644·000
235	197,400	12,337½	397,827	22·472	1·296	658·000
240	201,600	12,600	406,292	22·009	1·269	672·000
245	205,800	12,862½	414,756	21·560	1·243	686·000
250	210,000	13,125	423,221	21·129	1·919	700·000
255	214,200	13,387½	431,685	20·715	1·195	714·000
260	218,400	13,650	440,150	20·316	1·172	728·000
265	222,600	13,912½	448,614	19·933	1·150	742·000
270	226,800	14,175	457,078	19·564	1·128	756·000
275	231,000	14,437½	465,543	19·208	1·108	770·000
280	235,200	14,700	474,007	18·865	1·088	784·000
285	239,400	14,962½	482,472	18·534	1·069	798·000
290	243,600	15,225	490,936	18·214	1·050	812·000
295	247,800	15,487½	499,401	17·906	1·033	826·000
300	252,000	15,750	507,865	17·607	1·015	840·000
305	256,200	16,012½	516,329	17·319	0·999	854·000
310	260,400	16,275	524,794	17·039	0·983	868·000
315	264,600	16,537½	533,258	16·769	0·967	882·000
320	268,800	16,800	541,723	16·507	0·952	896·000
325	273,000	17,062½	550,187	16·253	0·937	910·000
330	277,200	17,325	558,652	16·007	0·923	924·000
335	281,400	17,587½	567,116	15·768	0·909	938·000
340	285,600	17,850	575,580	15·536	0·896	952·000
345	289,800	18,112½	584,045	15·311	0·883	966·000
350	294,000	18,375	592,509	15·092	0·870	980·000

Comparative Yarn Tables.

Cotton Scale.	Yards per lb.	Yards per oz.	Metres per Kilogramme.	Italian Scale in Deniers.	Manchester Scale. Drams per 1000 yds.	Linen Scale. Leas of 300 yds. in 1 lb.
355	298,200	18,637½	600,974	14·879	0·858	994·000
360	302,400	18,900	609,438	14·673	0·846	1,008·000
365	306,600	19,162½	617,903	14·472	0·834	1,022·000
370	310,800	19,425	626,367	14·276	0·823	1,036·000
375	315,000	19,687½	634,832	14·086	0·812	1,050·000
380	319,200	19,950	643,296	13·900	0·802	1,064·000
385	323,400	20,212½	651,761	13·720	0·791	1,078·000
390	327,600	20,475	660,225	13·544	0·781	1,092·000
395	331,800	20,737½	668,690	13·372	0·771	1,106·000
400	336,000	21,000	677,155	13·196	0·761	1,120·000
405	340,200	21,262½	685,619	13·042	0·752	1,134·000
410	344,400	21,525	694,082	12·883	0·743	1,148·000
415	348,600	21,787½	702,548	12·728	0·734	1,162·000
420	352,800	22,050	711,011	12·577	0·725	1,176·000
425	357,000	22,312½	719,477	12·428	0·717	1,190·000
430	361,200	22,575	727,940	12·284	0·708	1,204·000
435	365,400	22,837½	736,406	12·143	0·700	1,218·000
440	369,600	23,100	744,869	12·005	0·692	1,232·000
445	373,800	23,362½	753,334	11·870	0·684	1,246·000
450	378,000	23,625	761,797	11·738	0·677	1,260·000
455	382,200	23,887½	770,262	11·609	0·669	1,274·000
460	386,400	24,150	778,727	11·483	0·662	1,288·000
465	390,600	24,412½	787,191	11·359	0·655	1,302·000
470	394,800	24,675	795,655	11·236	0·648	1,316·000
475	399,000	24,937½	804,120	11·120	0·641	1,330·000
480	403,200	25,200	812,584	11·004	0·634	1,344·000
485	407,400	25,462½	821,048	10·891	0·628	1,358·000
490	411,600	25,725	829,513	10·780	0·621	1,372·000
495	415,800	25,987½	837,977	10·671	0·615	1,386·000
500	420,000	26,250	846,443	10·564	0·609	1,400·000
505	424,200	26,512½	854,906	10·460	0·603	1,414·000
510	428,400	26,775	863,371	10·357	0·597	1,428·000
515	432,600	27,037½	871,835	10·256	0·591	1,442·000
520	436,800	27,300	880,300	10·158	0·586	1,456·000
525	441,000	27,562½	888,764	10·061	0·580	1,470·000
530	445,200	27,825	897,229	9·966	0·575	1,484·000
535	449,400	28,087½	905,692	9·873	0·569	1,498·000
540	453,600	28,350	914,157	9·782	0·564	1,512·000
545	457,800	28,612½	922,621	9·692	0·559	1,526·000
550	462,000	28,875	931,086	9·604	0·554	1,540·000
555	466,200	29,137½	939,550	9·517	0·549	1,554·000
560	470,400	29,400	948,015	9·432	0·544	1,568·000
565	474,600	29,662½	956,479	9·349	0·539	1,582·000
570	478,800	29,925	964,944	9·267	0·534	1,596·000
575	483,000	30,187½	973,409	9·186	0·530	1,610·000
580	487,200	30,450	981,873	9·107	0·525	1,624·000
585	491,400	30,712½	990,338	9·029	0·520	1,638·000
590	495,600	30,975	998,802	8·953	0·516	1,652·000
595	499,800	31,237½	1,007,267	8·877	0·512	1,666·000
600	504,000	31,500	1,015,731	8·803	0·507	1,680·000

PRINCIPLES OF THE COUNTS.

Cotton Scale. The hank is 840 yds., and the number of such hanks in 1 lb. avoirdupois is the count of the yarn. The same scale is used for Patent Silk. $2/40^s$ Cotton means single 40^s doubled to 20^s; but $2/40^s$ Patent Silk (better written $40/2$ for distinction) is single 80^s doubled to 40^s. A spindle is 18 hanks = 15,120 yds.

Yards per lb. Is the most simple of all the scales.

Yards per oz. Is used in Dewsbury for Woollen yarn, and in Yorkshire generally for Organzine Silk, and is sometimes called the West of England scale.

Yds. per dram. Used in Huddersfield district for Woollen Yarn. "20 skein" yarn, means that 20 yds. will weigh 1 dram.

Metres per Kilogramme. French and Swiss No. 100^s. means 100,000 metres to the Kilogramme. This table is based on 1 metre = 39·370 inches, 1 Kilo. = 2·204 lbs.

Italian Scale. Authorities differ considerably as to the length of the hank, and the weight of a denier. We follow the rule of the London Silk Conditioning House, which is an acknowledged authority in all disputes. The hank is 400 French ells = 476 metres = 520 yards. $533\frac{1}{3}$ deniers make 1 oz avoirdupois. The number of deniers that one such hank weighs is the count of the yarn.

Manchester Scale. The hank is 1000 yds., and the number of drams that such a hank weighs is the count of the Yarn.

Linen Scale. The hank or Lea is 300 yds., and the number of these in 1 lb. is the count of the yarn. A spindle is 48 Leas = 14,400 yds. A bundle is 200 Leas = 60,000 yds.

Worsted Scale. The hank is 560 yds., and the number of such hanks in 1 lb. is the count of the yarn.

Hawick Scale. The Cut is 300 yds., and the number of Cuts in 26 oz. is the count of the yarn. A spindle is 48 cuts = 14,400 yds. A Slip is 12 Cuts.

Galashiels Scale. The Cut is 300 yds., and the number of Cuts in 24 oz. is the count of the yarn. A spindle is 48 cuts = 14,400 yds. A Slip is 12 Cuts.

Alloa Scale. Used also in Stirling, Kilmarnock and elsewhere. The Cut is 240 yds. 48 Cuts = 11,520 yds. make a spindle. The number of such spindles in 24 lb. is the count of the yarn.

Aberdeen Scale. The spindle is 14,400 yds., and the number of lbs. 2 spindle weighs is the count of the yarn. No 1^s or "1 lb. yarn" is 14,400 yds. to the lb.

JACQUARD CARD MACHINERY.

Regular and Fine Scale
PIANO MACHINES
and REPEATERS.

COMBINED
Punching and
Lacing Machines.

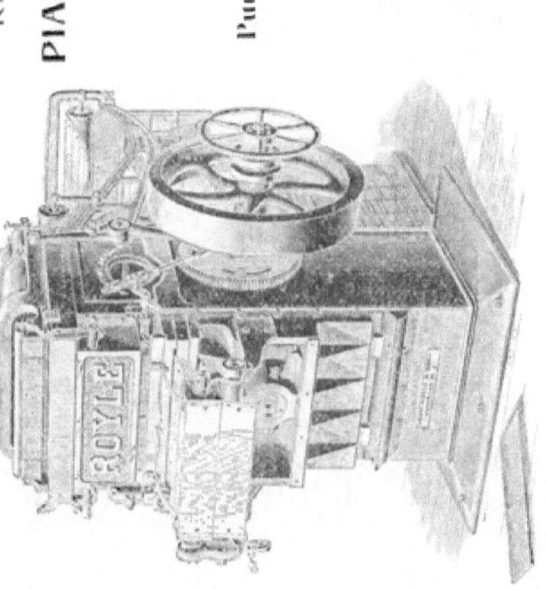

JOHN ROYLE & SONS,
PATERSON, N. J.

BUILDERS OF THE
LATEST MODERN IMPROVED

SILK MACHINERY

KENNEDY'S LATEST SWIVEL LOOM.

Winders, Power Warpers, Doublers, Quilling Frames, Broad Looms, Ribbon Looms, Ribbon Blockers. Silk Finishing Machinery and Throwing Machinery a Specialty. All Grades of Chemical, Ticker and Ribbon Paper Cut to any Desired Size and Properly Rolled. Pulleys, Hangers, Shafting and General Mill Wrights. Iron and Brass Foundry Attached. Estimates Cheerfully Given.

FRANKLIN MILLS, MILL ST., PATERSON, N. J.

www.ingramcontent.com/pod-product-compliance
Lightning Source LLC
Chambersburg PA
CBHW030340170426
43202CB00010B/1193